SIMPLY GOOD EATING

Underwood Road, Paisley, Scotland PA3 1TJ   041-887 1234
ISBN 0 903438 08 9

Photography by Graham Lees
Printed by Cambus Litho, East Kilbride

Simply Good Eating

BY
ELIZABETH MACINTOSH
ASSISTED BY
DIANE DUNCAN
AND
EILEEN MACPHEE

PUBLISHED BY
THE
SCOTTISH
MILK MARKETING
BOARD

Elizabeth MacIntosh, Diane Duncan, Eileen MacPhee
The Scottish Milk Marketing Board's Home Economists
at work in their dairy kitchen

Introduction

Good health is our most precious asset and is very important in the quality of our lives. Food can affect the quality of life and with this in mind, The Scottish Milk Marketing Board's Home Economists have compiled a selection of tempting recipes made from fresh Scottish food.

The dishes are quick and easy to prepare and use food in its most natural form. A wide variety of food should be eaten along with a healthy lifestyle including a sensible amount of exercise for your age and way of life.

Milk is the most complete of all foods and plays an important part in a well balanced diet. There is now a wide selection of milk available from your milkman or from shops, and on page 8 you will find further information to enable you to choose the milks which best suit your needs.

The first section in the book deals with the variety of dairy produce available and this is followed by the main recipe section which is a selection of dishes which will suit all occasions. They are all using fresh wholesome food and will fit into your healthy way of life.

Take a gastronomic tour around the world in the international section. Here you will find exciting and mouthwatering dishes which have been sent to us by Home Economists from ten countries in organisations similar to our own.

Microwave cookery is a modern means of cooking requiring new knowledge and skills. To help you to make more effective use of your oven, we have included a variety of recipes which are particularly successful.

The final section is step by step cooking for the young or inexperienced cook. This gives basic recipes which, once mastered, can open the door to greater culinary achievements.

HAPPY COOKING!

Contents

Milk

Milk is the only food which contains all the nutrients necessary to maintain life and promote body growth. Protein, fat, carbohydrates, mineral elements and vitamins are present in milk in well balanced proportions.

Nutrients per pint

	Whole	Semi-skimmed	Skimmed
Energy kcal	380	267	187
kJ	1,594	1,122	796
Protein g	18.9	19.5	19.8
Fat g	22.8	9.7	0.6
Carbohydrate g	26.8	27.0	27.3
Calcium mg	604	621	633
Iron mg	0.3	0.3	0.3
Sodium mg	293	299	305
Vitamin A (retinol equivalent) μg	330	140	9
Thiamin mg	0.26	0.27	0.28
Riboflavin mg	1.01	1.04	1.05
Niacin equivalent mg	5.0	5.1	5.2
Vitamin B$_{12}$ μg	2.5	2.5	2.6
Vitamin C mg	9[1]	9[1]	9[1]
Vitamin D μg	0.17	0.07	0

[1] Values decline on storage in the home.

Taken from 'Manual of Nutrition' eighth edition, published by Her Majesty's Stationery Office.

There is a wide variety of milks to choose from and the following information will help you to select the ones which most suit your needs.

Whole Milk — Containing less than 3.9% fat, whole milk is the most popular variety in Scotland and is available everywhere.

Semi-Skimmed Milk — This is milk which has had approximately half the fat removed giving a fat content of 1.5%-1.8%. Semi-skimmed is now widely available either from your milkman or from shops.

Skimmed Milk — This milk has had almost all the fat removed to produce a product which has a fat content of less than 0.3%. Availability in Scotland is improving but you may need to look for a local supplier.

Homogenised Milk — This is pasteurised milk which by means of forcing the milk through a very fine aperture, breaks down the fat globules and disperses them evenly through the milk.

Channel Islands Milk — Channel Islands milk must contain 4% butterfat and comes from Jersey or Guernsey cattle. It is not retailed widely in Scotland.

Sterilised Milk — Homogenised milk is filled into bottles which are capped with a metal cap and then the milk is heated to a temperature of not less than 100°C (212°F). There is little demand for this milk in Scotland.

U.H.T. Milk — The ultra heat treatment or 'Long Life' as it is sometimes called, is the process of heating homogenised milk to no less than 132°C (270°F) for at least one second and then cooled quickly and packaged in foil lined containers. It will keep for at least three months without refrigeration and is ideal for camping, sailing and as a reserve for your store cupboard.

Buttermilk — This is skimmed milk which has been pasteurised and then a special bacteria is added giving the buttermilk its distinctive taste.

The Care of Milk
Milk should be kept cool and covered at all times, preferably in a refrigerator.

Children and Milk
Young children need a good supply of energy as they are constantly running around. Whole milk is the best milk for them as it not only supplies them with a good amount of calcium, vitamins and minerals but it is also an easily consumed food with a good supply of calories. A government report in 1985 — The Committee on Medical Aspects of Food Policy (COMA) — recommended that children below the age of five be given whole cows milk.

There are many ways to encourage children to take milk — in cereals, porridge, hot drinks, soup, rice, milk jelly and puddings. If a child does not like milk to drink on its own, a flavour can be added for their enjoyment to give a drink which will still give them the nutritional value of milk.

Fresh cream is one of the good things in life so don't be persuaded to use a substitute. Cream is obtained from fresh milk and has no additives or preservatives.

Cream is a very versatile food and can be used for sweet or savoury dishes. There are lots of interesting recipes further on in the book for you to try out.

Types of cream are defined by the percentage of butterfat in them and the legal requirements are as follows:

Half Cream	12%
Single Cream	18%
Whipping Cream	35%
Double Cream	48%
Clotted Cream	55%

Uses of Cream

Half Cream — This is a thin pouring cream which is used for coffee or for pouring over sweets or cereals.

Single Cream — Single cream is homogenised to prevent separation and it may be pasteurised. It can be used for pouring and may be added to sauces. It will not whip.

Whipping Cream — As the name suggests this cream will whip and can be used for filling cakes and piping cream on trifles and cakes. It can also be used in sauces, for pouring, and for making ice cream.

Double Cream — Double cream can be used in the same ways as whipping and pouring cream. It has a high fat content and this means it will whip more quickly and form a denser cream than whipping and will retain its shape longer after being used for piping or decoration.

Soured Cream — This is a single cream which has a culture added to it to give a piquant flavour and a thick texture. It can be used for sweet or savoury dishes. If you want to make your own soured cream, add a teaspoon of lemon juice to a 140ml ($\frac{1}{4}$ pint) carton of single cream.

Crème Fraiche — This product is now made from Scottish milk and can be used in any recipe using soured cream. It is ideal for cheesecakes.

Long Life Cream — This cream also called Ultra Heat Treated (U.H.T.) cream, comes in three types, single, whipping and double and can be used in place of its fresh counterpart. The cream is heat treated to enable it to be kept not necessarily under refrigeration for up to twelve weeks.

U.H.T. milk and cream are handy to have in your cupboard in an emergency should you run short of fresh at any time.

Storage of Fresh Cream

Fresh cream should be kept in its original container. It should be kept cool, preferably in a refrigerator and covered and kept away from strong flavours.

How to Whip Cream for Best Results

The cream, bowl and whisk should be really cold. Whip the cream quickly at first with a fork, balloon whisk or rotary whisk and when it begins to thicken and take on a matt finish, beat more slowly until it stands in peaks. An electric mixer is not recommended as it is difficult not to overbeat the cream.

Scottish Cheese

Cheese is one of the most versatile foods available. It can be eaten at any meal, at any time and there is a great variety of Scottish cheese available, from the soft cottage cheese which is very popular in salads, mixed with other ingredients, to the very versatile Scottish cheddar cheese for which there are literally hundreds of uses. There are very few savoury recipes which cannot be topped up with the addition of grated cheddar cheese. It is an ideal snack for small children, and is an excellent source of calcium and energy.

There is no waste with cheese and you can buy the amount which you require of any number of different types. Care should be taken when storing it, depending on the types, but generally it is best to wrap cheese loosely and keep it in a fridge. Before eating it, it is best to take the cheese out of the fridge for at least half an hour, to enable it to come to room temperature gradually so that you can enjoy its full flavour. In storing, cheese looses none of its food value and if properly stored, there should be no waste.

As a food, cheese is excellent for the elderly as small amounts can be bought, and it will keep for several days and there is no danger of it going bad. It is an excellent source of first class protein.

In the main recipe section, you will find many recipes using Scottish cheddar cheese and some of the soft cheese; try them out and enjoy yourself!

Yogurt

Yogurt has long been a traditional food of the people of the Balkans and the Middle East. It has been used for centuries for its therapeutic qualities and the medical profession recognise its use in cases of minor intestinal ailments.

Yogurt has had a great success story in this country in the last twenty years. It is widely bought in a great variety of flavours and types. Natural yogurt is very versatile and gives a unique flavour to a sauce. Other types of yogurt are set, stirred, flavoured, fruit, low fat and very low fat.

Greek Style Yogurt is a yogurt with a tangy flavour which will enhance salads and savoury dishes. It is easy to use and despite its name, it is now available made from Scottish milk.

Home Made Soft Yogurt

560ml (1 pint) pasteurised milk
1 teaspoon sugar (if further sweetening e.g. jam or honey is not used)
140ml (¼ pint) natural yogurt

Method
1. Warm the milk to blood heat (36°C/98°F).
2. Remove from heat and stir in sugar.
3. Gently whisk in yogurt with a wire whisk or a fork.
4. Transfer to a bowl and cover.
5. Leave in a warm place or in a vacuum flask for 8-12 hours, or until set.
6. If cold yogurt is preferred refrigerate after setting.

Yield

Approximately ¾ litre (1¼ pints).

Once the yogurt has set it is ready for use, either as it is or with the addition of fruit or flavouring.

For firmer yogurt use U.H.T. milk.

For low fat yogurt use skimmed milk with 1 dessertspoon instant milk powder added when warm.

For flavoured yogurt add either a fruit flavour or jam to add a touch of colour to the yogurt. The addition of a dessertspoon of honey makes a delicious yogurt. For fruit yogurt add small pieces of fresh, canned or thawed frozen fruit.

Interesting combinations can be made — chocolate and mint or coffee and walnut. You can add the flavouring before or after the yogurt is made. If you add the flavouring after the yogurt is made every member of the family can have his or her favourite flavour.

Flavourings

To add to your home made soft yogurt

Fresh fruit	100g (4oz)
Blackcurrant of fresh orange juice	2-3 tablespoons
Milk shake flavouring	2 tablespoons
Coffee and cocoa powder	1 tablespoon
Essence	to taste
Nuts	to taste
Sweetener (if wanted)	
Sugar	1 tablespoon ⎤
Honey	1 tablespoon ⎬ add after yogurt is made
Syrup	1 tablespoon ⎦

Butter

There is nothing to compare with the flavour of butter; it is made from cream which has been churned and it may have a little salt added to it. Butter is a whole food and contains no chemicals.

If you are watching your fat intake make sure that what you take is worth eating, i.e. that it has the best flavour and that it is natural.

There are many ways in which butter can be served, some of these are illustrated here.

Freezing of Dairy Produce

The best way to use dairy products is in a fresh state but if you wish to store some for a while, here are some tips in deep freezing them.

Milk
Homogenised milk can be frozen for up to one month in a plastic container — never freeze a liquid in a glass container. If you have too much of any other kind of milk, make the milk into a sauce or sweet and freeze in that form.

Cream
Single cream does not freeze well but whipping or double cream will freeze best if you whip it lightly and add a little sugar. If you have cream left over when piping a cake, pipe the excess onto a metal tray. Freeze the cream in rosettes and then store in a plastice box or bag in the freezer and use as required, they take very little time to defrost when required.

Cheese
Cheddar cheese retains a good flavour after freezing although it tends to crumble after it is thawed. Cheese can be grated before freezing and used as required in small amounts. Soft cheeses tend to become stronger in flavour after freezing.

Butter
Butter freezes well and should be double wrapped before freezing.

Yogurt
Yogurt may separate out after thawing but a stir with a spoon will rectify this.

Any foods to be frozen should be well covered, especially dairy produce, to avoid any transfer of flavours during freezing.

Citrus Carrot Soup

50g (2oz) butter
1 onion, finely chopped
450g (1lb) carrots, diced
225g ($\frac{1}{2}$lb) potatoes, diced
1 teaspoon rosemary
560ml (1 pint) stock
840ml (1$\frac{1}{2}$ pints) milk
75g (3oz) Scottish cheddar cheese, grated
seasoning
juice of 1 orange

Serves 4-6
Method
1. Melt butter. Cook onions gently.
2. Add carrots, potatoes, sauté and add stock. Season.
3. Bring to boil. Add milk.
4. Simmer uncovered for 30 minutes or until carrots are soft.
5. Liquidise. Add orange juice.
6. Reheat then stir in grated cheese and serve immediately.

Cream of Cauliflower Soup

25g (1oz) butter
1 onion, chopped
2 syboes, chopped
25g (1oz) wholemeal flour
560ml (1 pint) milk
280ml ($\frac{1}{2}$ pint) water
seasoning
1 large cauliflower, washed and separated into florets
70ml ($\frac{1}{8}$ pint) double cream

Serves 6
Method
1. Melt butter in a large saucepan. Add onion and syboes and cook for 2 minutes.
2. Stir in wholemeal flour and cook for a further minute then gradually stir in milk and water. Season.
3. Add cauliflower florets and cook for 30 minutes.
4. Liquidise soup and stir in cream — heat through gently but do not boil.
5. Serve hot with crusty bread or croûtons.

Creamy Corn Chowder

50g (2oz) butter
1 small onion, chopped
2 sticks celery, chopped
50g (2oz) plain flour
1 litre (2 pints) milk
1 chicken stock cube
1×335g (11oz) tin sweetcorn
140ml ($\frac{1}{4}$ pint) single cream
100g (4oz) cottage cheese
chopped parsley to garnish

Serves 6-8
Method
1. Melt butter in saucepan. Sauté onion and celery until soft.
2. Add flour, gradually stir in milk, add chicken stock cube.
3. Cook and stir over a medium heat until the mixture comes to the boil.
4. Add corn, cream and cottage cheese.
5. Reheat but do not boil.
6. Garnish with chopped parsley.

Chilled Tomato Soup

450g (1lb) tomatoes
140ml ($\frac{1}{4}$ pint) natural yogurt
1 teaspoon sugar
pinch salt
1 tablespoon worcester sauce
1 tablespoon lemon juice
140 ml ($\frac{1}{4}$ pint) single cream

Serves **4**
Method
1. Skin tomatoes (place in boiling water for $\frac{1}{2}$ minute, drain and peel).
2. Place tomatoes and all other ingredients except cream in blender. Blend till smooth.
3. Strain soup to remove pips. Stir in cream.
4. Chill. Then garnish with parsley.

Creamy Leek and Potato Soup

25g (1oz) butter
225g (8oz) leeks, sliced
225g (8oz) potatoes, diced
1 onion, finely chopped
840ml (1$\frac{1}{2}$ pints) stock
2 teaspoons ground coriander
pinch salt
140ml ($\frac{1}{4}$ pint) single cream

Serves **4**
Method
1. Melt butter, sauté onions, leeks and potatoes.
2. Add stock. Bring to boil.
3. Season.
4. Simmer for 30 minutes.
5. Add cream just before serving.

Hummus

225g (8oz) chickpeas, soaked overnight

2 cloves garlic, peeled and crushed

75g (3oz) tahini (sesame seed paste)

2 teaspoons salt

3 tablespoons double cream

juice of 2 lemons

parsley to garnish

Method

1. Rinse chickpeas with cold water then place in a saucepan and cover with cold water.

2. Bring to boil, then simmer for about 1 hour. Drain and rinse with cold water.

3. Liquidise to make a thick purée. Add water as necessary.

4. Place purée in a bowl and stir in all other ingredients.

5. Place in serving dish. Garnish with radish and serve with pitta bread and crudités as photograph.

Vegetable Patch Dip

225g (8oz) cottage cheese

2 tablespoons mayonnaise

2 tablespoons natural yogurt

1 small carrot, grated

1 small onion, finely chopped

1 tablespoon parsley, finely chopped

seasoning

garnish with grated carrot and cress

Method

1. Combine cottage cheese, mayonnaise and natural yogurt in a bowl.

2. Stir in carrot, onion and parsley. Season to taste.

3. Spoon into a serving dish and chill.

4. Serve garnished with carrot and cress. Delicious with hot buttered toast.

Tuna Party Spread

200g (7oz) can tuna, drained & flaked
225g (8oz) cream cheese
1 small onion, very finely chopped
2 tablespoons lemon juice
1 teaspoon worcester sauce
seasoning

Method
1. Beat together tuna and cheese. Stir in onions, lemon juice and worcester sauce.
2. Season to taste.
3. Transfer into a serving dish. Cover and chill.
4. Garnish with parsley and serve with crackers.

Spreading Forest Fire Dip

100g (4oz) smooth cottage cheese
4 tablespoons double cream
2 tablespoons mayonnaise
1 teaspoon worcester sauce
1 teaspoon garlic salt
$\frac{1}{2}$ teaspoon cayenne pepper
1 green chilli, very finely chopped

Method
1. Place cottage cheese in a bowl and beat to soften.
2. Add double cream, mayonnaise, worcester sauce, garlic salt and cayenne pepper. Mix until smooth.
3. Add chilli and stir to blend.
4. Pour into serving dish and chill.
5. Garnish with a little paprika pepper before serving with fresh vegetables and crackers.

Braemar Salmon

1 ripe avocado pear
2 tablespoons lemon juice
$\frac{1}{4}$-$\frac{1}{2}$ honeydew melon, sliced
100g (4oz) smoked salmon (4 slices)
70ml ($\frac{1}{8}$ pint) double cream
1 tablespoon mayonnaise
1 tablespoon tomato ketchup
seasoning
lemon to garnish

Serves **4**

Method

1. Slice avocado and dip in lemon juice.

2. Roll a slice of melon and avocado in each piece of smoked salmon.

3. Place the rolls on serving dishes.

4. Lightly whip double cream. Add mayonnaise and tomato ketchup. Season.

5. Pour sauce over smoked salmon rolls.

6. Serve with two slices of avocado and two of melon. Garnish with a slice of lemon.

Curried Crinan Prawns

25g (1oz) butter

25g (1oz) plain flour

1-2 teaspoons curry powder

140ml (¼ pint) milk

140ml (¼ pint) single cream

seasoning

225g (8oz) peeled prawns

100g (4oz) long grain rice

parsley to garnish

Oven temperature: 170°C/325°F/No. 4
Position in oven: Top
Time in oven: 10 minutes (approx)
Serves 4
Method

1. In a saucepan melt butter then add the flour and curry powder. Cook for 1 minute.

2. Remove from the heat and gradually add the milk and then the cream.

3. Cook over a gentle heat until sauce thickens.

4. Season and stir in prawns.

5. Place mixture in individual ovenproof dishes.

6. Bake until top is browned. Serve with boiled rice.

Smoked Haddock Creams

225g (8oz) smoked haddock

½ onion, finely chopped

75g (3oz) butter

140ml (¼ pint) white sauce, cold

2 teaspoons lemon juice

seasoning

140ml (¼ pint) double cream

4 slices lemon, to garnish

4 slices cucumber, to garnish

Method

1. Fry haddock with onion in 25g (1oz) butter, then liquidise.

2. Mix haddock, remaining butter, white sauce, lemon juice and seasoning together.

3. Whip cream stiffly then fold in haddock mixture.

4. Divide amongst 4 ramekin dishes and smooth top. Garnish with twist of lemon and cucumber.

5. Serve with hot buttered fingers of toast.

Peanut Palmiers

225g (8oz) plain flour	

225g (8oz) plain flour

pinch salt

$\frac{1}{2}$ teaspoon dry mustard

100g (4oz) butter, softened

100g (4oz) Scottish cheddar cheese, grated

1 egg, lightly beaten

75g (3oz) salted peanuts, chopped finely

Oven temperature: 200°C/400°F/No. 6
Position in oven: Top
Time in oven: 10-15 minutes
Makes **30** Palmiers
Method
1. *Pastry* — sift flour, salt and mustard into a bowl. Rub in the butter until the mixture resembles breadcrumbs.
2. Stir in grated cheese. Add $\frac{1}{2}$ the beaten egg and enough cold water to mix to a firm dough. Wrap pastry and chill for $\frac{1}{2}$ hour before rolling out.
3. *Palmiers* — roll out cheese pastry to a 30cm (12 inch) square. Brush with remaining egg. Sprinkle with peanuts.
4. Roll opposite sides of square into the centre, towards each other. Press firmly together.
5. Cut into 30 slices using a sharp knife.
6. Arrange slices, cut sides up on a baking tray and flatten slightly.
7. Bake. Serve hot or cold.

Cheesy Bitelets

100g (4oz) butter

150g (6oz) Scottish cheddar cheese, finely grated

pinch dry mustard

salt and pepper

1 small onion, finely chopped

1 dessertspoon tomato ketchup

50g (2oz) walnuts, finely chopped

parsley, finely chopped

Method
1. Cream butter and cheddar cheese together.
2. Add mustard, seasoning, onion and tomato ketchup. Mix well.
3. Form the mixture into approximately 30 small balls. Roll in a mixture of parsley and walnuts. Delicious served with a drink before dinner.

Hot Cheese Crispers

75g (3oz) smooth cottage cheese

2 tablespoons milk

1 tablespoon flour

1 tablespoon tomato ketchup

1 tablespoon curry powder

salt and pepper

24 small crisp biscuits or pieces of toast

25g (1oz) bacon flavoured crisps, crushed

paprika

Method
1. Combine the cottage cheese with milk, flour, tomato ketchup, curry powder and seasoning.
2. Spread the mixture onto the biscuits.
3. Sprinkle the top with crisps and a little paprika pepper.
4. Place the biscuits on a baking tray and place under a hot grill for 2-3 minutes, until crispy.
5. Serve hot with drinks.

Sesame Cheese Bites

100g (4oz) wholemeal flour	
100g (4oz) plain flour	
$\frac{1}{2}$ teaspoon baking powder	
pinch salt	pastry
$\frac{1}{2}$ teaspoon dry mustard powder	
100g (4oz) butter	
100g (4oz) Scottish cheddar cheese, grated	
1 egg, lightly beaten	
25g (1oz) sesame seeds	filling

Oven temperature: 200°C/400°F/No. 6
Position in oven: Top
Time in oven: 10-15 minutes
Makes approximately **40**
Method
1. *Pastry* — place wholemeal flour in a bowl. Sieve in plain flour, baking powder, salt and mustard.
2. Rub in butter until the mixture resembles breadcrumbs.
3. Stir in grated cheese. Add $\frac{1}{2}$ the egg and a little cold water to mix to a firm dough. Chill for 30 minutes.
4. *Bites* — Roll out pastry to a 30cm (12 inch) square. Brush with remaining egg and sprinkle with sesame seeds.
5. Cut pastry into strips 2cm (1 inch) wide then cut strips diagonally to form diamond shapes.
6. Place shapes on a baking sheet and bake. Cool and serve.

Mushroom Courgette Quiche

150g (6oz) wholemeal flour	
pinch salt	
½ teaspoon baking powder	pastry
75g (3oz) butter	
3-4 tablespoons milk	
25g (1oz) butter	
1 onion, finely chopped	
2 courgettes, sliced	
150g (6oz) mushrooms, thinly sliced	filling
seasoning	
140ml (¼ pint) milk	
2 (size 3) eggs	
50g (2oz) Scottish cheddar cheese	

Garnish with sliced mushrooms

Oven temperature: Pastry 180°C/350°F/
No. 4 for 15 minutes
Quiche 200°C/400°F/
No. 6 for 25-30 minutes

Position in oven: Top

Serves **6-8**

Method

1. *Pastry* — sieve dry ingredients together. Rub butter into flour.
2. Add milk gradually to form a soft dough.
3. Refrigerate for 10 minutes then roll out and line a 20cm (8 inch) flan ring. Bake blind.
4. *Filling* — melt butter in a frying pan. Add the onion and fry for 5 minutes. Add courgettes and fry until lightly browned.
5. Stir in the mushrooms and seasoning. Mix well and cool.
6. Mix milk, eggs and cheese together then add the courgette mixture. Pour into flan case.
7. Bake until golden brown or filling is firm.

Cauliflower Quiche

150g (6oz) wholemeal flour	
pinch salt	
½ teaspoon baking powder	wholemeal pastry
75g (3oz) butter	
3-4 tablespoons milk	
450g (1lb) cauliflower florets	
25g (1oz) butter	
225g (8oz) onions, skinned and chopped	filling
25g (1oz) flour	
280ml (½ pint milk)	
seasoning	
100g (4 oz) Scottish cheddar cheese, grated	

Oven temperature: Pastry 180°C/350°F/
No. 4 for 15 minutes
Quiche 190°C/375°F/
No. 5 for 25-30 minutes

Position in oven: Top

Serves **4-6**

Method

1. *Pastry* — sieve dry ingredients together. Rub butter into flour.
2. Add milk gradually to form a soft dough.
3. Refrigerate for 10 minutes, then roll out and line a 20cm (8 inch) flan ring. Bake blind for 15 minutes.
4. Cook the cauliflower florets in a saucepan of boiling water for 5 minutes until just tender. Drain well and cool.
5. *Filling* — melt butter and gently fry onions until soft. Add flour and cook 1-2 minutes. Gradually add milk, stirring continuously until the sauce thickens. Season well.
6. Sprinkle half the Scottish cheddar cheese over the base of the pastry case. Arrange cauliflower florets on top.
7. Pour over onion sauce and sprinkle over remaining Scottish cheddar cheese.
8. Bake for 25-30 minutes. Serve and garnish with parsley if desired.

Tuna Fish Cheesecake

100g (4oz) plain biscuits	
50g (2oz) butter	base
25g (1oz) Scottish cheddar cheese, grated	

15g (½ oz) butter	
1 onion, finely chopped	
2 tomatoes, peeled and chopped	
1 teaspoon basil	
200g (7oz) tin tuna fish, well drained and flaked	filling
juice and rind of 1 lemon	
100g (4oz) smooth cottage cheese	
140ml (¼ pint) double cream, lightly whipped	

Serves **6-8**

Method

1. *Base* — melt butter, add biscuit crumbs and cheese. Press into a 15cm (6 inch) loose bottomed cake tin. Chill.
2. *Filling* — melt butter. Gently sauté onion.
3. Add tomatoes, seasoning, tuna fish and lemon. Mix well and leave to cool and drain.
4. Blend cottage cheese until smooth.
5. Add savoury mixture. Mix well.
6. Gently mix in lightly whipped cream.
7. Spoon the mixture over the base and chill until firm.
8. Decorate.

Vegetable Lasagne

150g (6oz) lasagne verdi
1 tablespoon vegetable oil
50g (2oz) butter
1 onion, finely chopped
1 clove garlic, crushed
1 red pepper, chopped
1 green pepper, chopped
225g (8oz) courgettes, sliced
100g (4oz) mushrooms, sliced
100g (4oz) baked beans
400g (14½oz) tin tomatoes
1 tablespoon tomato purée
1 teaspoon basil
1 teaspoon oregano
100g (4oz) Scottish cheddar cheese, grated ⎫
40g (1½oz) butter ⎬ cheese sauce
40g (1½oz) flour ⎪
420ml (¾ pint) milk ⎭
25g (1oz) Scottish cheddar cheese, grated — topping

Oven temperature	180°C/350°F/No. 4
Position in oven:	Centre
Time in oven:	30 minutes

Serves **4**
Method
1. Cook lasagne according to direction on packet.
2. Melt butter. Gently fry onion and garlic.
3. Add peppers, courgettes, mushrooms, baked beans, tomatoes, tomato purée, herbs and seasoning. Mix well.
4. *Sauce* — melt butter, blend in flour and gradually blend in milk. Bring to boil stirring all the time. Cook for 2-3 minutes. Add cheese.
5. Cover casserole dish first with layer of lasagne. Add a layer of vegetables then pour over sauce. Repeat, finishing with layer of sauce.
6. Sprinkle cheese on top. Bake in oven.

Cottage Hot Pot

15g (½oz) butter
1 large onion, chopped
225g (8oz) tagliatelle, cooked
25g (1oz) butter ⎫
25g (1oz) wholemeal flour ⎪
280ml (½ pint) milk ⎪
seasoning ⎬ sauce
100g (4oz) Scottish cheddar cheese, grated ⎪
225g (8oz) cottage cheese ⎭
50g (2oz) salted peanuts
1 tablespoon tomato purée

Oven temperature:	190°C/350°F/No. 5
Position in oven:	Top
Time in oven:	20-25 minutes

Serves **4**
Method
1. Melt butter and fry onion.
2. *Sauce* — melt butter, add flour and cook for one minute. Gradually add milk and cook until mixture thickens. Season and add half the Scottish cheddar cheese and half the cottage cheese. Add onions.
3. Stir in peanuts and add tomato purée.
4. Combine sauce and tagliatelle.
5. Place mixture in an ovenproof dish. Sprinkle with remaining cheese.
6. Bake until golden brown.

Savoury Cheese and Nut Loaf

100g (4oz) self raising flour
100g (4oz) wholemeal flour
100g (4oz) wholemeal breadcrumbs
100g (4 oz) butter
also 15g (½oz) butter to sauté onions
100g (4oz) mixed nuts
150g (6oz) Scottish cheddar cheese, grated
100g (4oz) onions, finely chopped
1 teaspoon mixed herbs
2 eggs, beaten
140ml (¼ pint) milk

Oven temperature: 180°C/350°F/No. 4
Position in oven: Centre
Time in oven: 1½ hours + 15 minutes
Serves **6**

Method
1. Rub 100g (4oz) butter into flour until it resembles fine breadcrumbs.
2. Add wholemeal breadcrumbs, nuts, cheese and seasoning. Mix well.
3. Sauté onion and add to dry ingredients.
4. Add the eggs and enough milk to bind the ingredients together.
5. Pour mixture into a lightly greased 1kg (2lb) loaf tin.
6. Cover with foil and bake for 1½ hours.
7. Remove foil and continue baking for 15 minutes.
8. Allow to cool in tin before turning out onto a wire rack.
9. Serve with a green salad.

Scone Pizza

100g (4oz) self raising flour

pinch salt

1 rounded teaspoon baking powder

100g (4oz) wholemeal flour

40g (1½oz) butter

50g (2oz) Scottish cheddar cheese, grated

8-10 tablespoons milk

25g (1oz) butter ⎤

1 onion, chopped

150g (6oz) mushrooms, sliced

200g (7oz) tin tomatoes, drained ⎬ topping

2 teaspoons mixed herbs

seasoning

150g (6oz) Scottish cheddar
cheese, grated ⎦

Oven temperature: 210°C/425°F/No. 7
Position in oven: Centre
Time in oven: 25-30 minutes
No. of servings: **16 slices**
Method
1. Sieve self raising flour, salt and baking powder into a bowl. Stir in wholemeal flour.
2. Rub in butter. Stir in cheese.
3. Add milk to form a soft but not sticky dough. Knead lightly.
4. On a lightly floured surface, roll pizza dough out to fit a lightly greased 23cm × 30cm (9 inch × 12 inch) baking sheet.
5. *Topping* — in a frying pan melt butter, add onion and cook until soft. Stir in mushrooms, tomatoes, herbs and seasoning. Leave to cool.

6. Place topping on base, sprinkle with cheese and bake.

Potato Pizza

150g (6oz) potatoes

50g (2oz) butter

25g (1oz) syboes, chopped finely

75g (3oz) self raising flour

75g (3oz) wholemeal flour

1 rounded teaspoon baking powder

seasoning

25g (1oz) butter ⎤

1 small green pepper, chopped

1 garlic clove, crushed

200g (7oz) tin tomatoes, drained

seasoning ⎬ topping

1 teaspoon basil

75g (3oz) salami or garlic
sausage

75g (3oz) Scottish cheddar cheese

4 olives, halved and stoned ⎦

Oven temperature: 210°C/425°F/No. 7
Position in oven: Centre
Time in oven: 25-30 minutes
Serves **4**
Method
1. *Base* — boil potatoes. Drain and mash with the butter, mix in syboes.
2. Stir in flours, baking powder and seasoning to form a soft dough.

3. Knead lightly then roll out dough to form a 20cm (8 inch) circle. Carefully transfer onto a lightly buttered baking sheet.
4. *Topping* — melt butter in a frying pan add green pepper and garlic and cook until pepper is soft.
5. Stir in tomatoes and basil, season. Cool.
6. Place topping on pizza base. Arrange salami, cheese and olives on top and bake.

Cheesy Corn Puff

425g (15oz) can sweetcorn
50g (2oz) butter
1 small onion, finely chopped
50g (2oz) plain flour
280ml ($\frac{1}{2}$ pint) milk
150g (6oz) Scottish cheddar cheese, grated
2 (size 3) eggs, separated
seasoning

Oven temperature: 180°C/350°F/No. 4
Position in oven: Centre
Time in oven: 40-45 minutes
Serves **4-6**
Method
1. Drain corn and leave aside.
2. Melt butter in a saucepan. Sauté onion until soft. Blend in flour. Gradually stir in milk. Cook and bring to the boil.
3. Remove from the heat and add cheese. Stir until melted.

4. Add corn, egg yolks and seasoning.
5. Whisk egg whites until stiff and fold into corn mixture.
6. Pour into a 1 litre (2 pint) casserole or soufflé dish.
7. Bake. Serve immediately.

Cheesy Mustard Drumsticks

8 chicken drumsticks
75g (3oz) Scottish cheddar cheese, grated
75g (3oz) rolled oats
1 tablespoon mustard powder
seasoning
50g (2oz) plain flour
2 (size 3) eggs, lightly beaten
50g (2oz) butter

Oven temperature: 200°C/400°F/No. 6
Position in oven: Centre
Time in oven: 45-50 minutes
Serves **4**
Method
1. Remove skin from chicken drumsticks.
2. Mix together Scottish cheddar cheese, rolled oats, mustard powder and seasoning.
3. Dip drumsticks in plain flour then in beaten egg and finally in the cheese and oat mixture.
4. Place on a baking sheet and dot with butter.
5. Bake until chicken is crisp and tender.

Tuna Mushroom Bannock

100g (4oz) wholemeal flour
100g (4oz) self raising flour
1 level teaspoon baking powder
pinch salt
50g (2oz) butter
1 (size 3) egg, beaten
5-6 tablespoon milk (approx)

25g (1oz) butter	
50g (2oz) mushrooms, sliced	
75g (3oz) tin tuna fish, drained	filling
100g (4oz) Scottish cheddar cheese, grated	
2 tablespoons milk	

Oven temperature: 230°C/450°F/No. 8
Position in oven: Top
Time in oven: 10-15 minutes
Serves **6**

Method

1. Place wholemeal flour in a bowl. Sieve in self raising flour, baking powder and salt. Rub in butter.

2. Mix in egg and milk to make a soft dough. Turn mixture out onto a floured surface. Knead lightly into a round about 18cm (7 inch) in diameter.

3. Place on a buttered baking sheet, dust with flour and score into 6 sections. Bake until well risen and golden brown.

4. *To make filling* — Fry the mushrooms in 15g (½oz) butter until soft. Beat remaining butter, cheese and milk together to make a smooth paste. Mix in mushrooms and tuna.

5. Split bannock in half and fill with the mixture. Serve hot or cold.

Creamy Vegetable Plait

200g (8oz) puff pastry

15g (½oz) butter	
15g (½oz) wholemeal flour	
140ml (¼ pint) milk	
75g (3oz) Scottish cheddar cheese, grated	
seasoning	
½ small cauliflower, separated into florets	filling
1 small onion, chopped	
75g (3oz) mushrooms, sliced	
75g (3oz) sweetcorn	
milk to glaze	

Oven temperature: 200°C/400°F/No. 6
Position in oven: Top
Time in oven: 25-30 minutes
Serves **4-6**

Method

1. Roll out pastry into a rectangle 25cm × 30 cm (10 inch × 12 inch).

2. *Filling* — melt butter in a saucepan, add flour and cook for 1 minute. Gradually add milk, bring to boil and cook until sauce thickens. Stir in cheese and season. Remove from heat.

3. Mix in prepared vegetables and allow mixture to cool.

4. Lightly mark pastry into three, lengthwise. Place on a baking sheet and cut slits at a 45° angle downwards on the outside thirds. Keep the strips about 2cm (1 inch) apart.

5. Place filling down the centre. Brush the strips with milk. Fold ends up over filling and lift strips alternately over one another. Brush with milk and bake.

Bow-ties Italiano

450g (1lb) bow-tie shaped pasta

450g (1lb) lean minced beef

$\frac{1}{2}$ green pepper, chopped

$\frac{1}{2}$ red pepper, chopped

1 × 425g (15oz) can cream of chicken soup

100g (4oz) Scottish cheddar cheese, grated

140ml ($\frac{1}{4}$ pint) milk

100g (4oz) sweetcorn

1 teaspoon oregano

1 teaspoon basil

1 teaspoon marjoram

1 tablespoon parmesan cheese

peppers to garnish

Serves **4-6**

Method

1. Cook pasta according to package directions, drain well, leave aside.

2. Brown minced beef, add green and red pepper and sauté for 10-15 minutes until cooked.

3. Combine soup, cheese, milk, corn and herbs in a saucepan. Cook and stir until cheese melts and sauce is heated.

4. Stir in meat mixture and macaroni, reheat if necessary.

5. Serve sprinkled with parmesan and garnished with pepper rings.

Peppered Pork and Ginger Casserole

340g (12oz) diced pork	
1 onion, chopped	
1 green pepper, chopped	
25g (1oz) butter	
40g (1½oz) plain flour	
140ml (¼ pint) chicken stock	
140ml (¼ pint) milk	
75g (3oz) sweetcorn	
1 medium cooking apple, peeled and chopped	
100g (4oz) mushrooms, quartered	
1 dessertspoon worcester sauce	
2 level teaspoons ground ginger	
3 tablespoons double cream	
seasoning	
50g (2oz) Scottish cheddar cheese, grated	} topping
25g (1oz) potato crisps, crushed	

Oven temperature: 190°C/375°F/No. 5
Position in oven: Top
Time in oven: 40-45 minutes
Serves **4**
Method
1. Melt butter in a frying pan. Add pork and brown. Add onion, green pepper and cook until soft.
2. Stir in flour, cook for 1-2 minutes.
3. Add remaining casserole ingredients and transfer into an ovenproof dish. Cover and cook for 30 minutes.
4. Remove from oven, stir in cream then sprinkle over mixed cheese and crisps. Return to oven for the remaining cooking time.
5. Serve on a bed of rice and garnish with parsley.

Somerset Baked Chicken

75g (3oz) butter
340g (12oz) uncooked chicken, cubed
1 large onion, chopped
50g (2oz) plain flour
420ml (¾ pint) chicken stock
280ml (½ pint) dry cider
seasoning
150g (6oz) mushrooms, sliced
3 tablespoons chopped parsley
140ml (¼ pint) single cream

Oven temperature: 190°C/375°F/No. 5
Position in oven: Top
Time in oven: 30-40 minutes
Serves **4**
Method
1. Melt 25g (1oz) butter and gently fry chicken and onion for 3-4 minutes. Remove from pan and place in a casserole.
2. Melt remaining butter and stir in flour gradually, add stock and cider, stirring continuously to make a smooth sauce. Season well.
3. Add mushrooms and 2 tablespoons of chopped parsley.
4. Pour sauce over chicken and onion. Cover and cook for 30-40 minutes.
5. Just before serving stir in the cream and garnish with 1 tablespoon parsley.
6. Serve hot with roast potatoes and vegetables.

Tagliatelle Carbonara

4 (size 3) eggs
140ml (¼ pint) double cream
25g (1oz) butter
225g (8oz) streaky bacon, chopped
350g (12oz) tagliatelle
150g (6oz) Scottish cheddar cheese, grated
salt and freshly ground pepper
chopped parsley to garnish

Serves **4**
Method
1. In a bowl, beat together eggs and cream.
2. Melt the butter in a frying pan and fry the bacon until crisp.
3. Meanwhile, cook the tagliatelle until just tender but not soft.
4. Drain and add it to the bacon in the frying pan.
5. Cook for 1 minute stirring all the time. Remove from heat and add egg mixture. Mix well.
6. Stir in 100g (4oz) cheese and season. Transfer to a serving dish and serve immediately, sprinkled with cheese and parsley.

Cyprus Chicken

25g (1oz) butter

2 tablespoons oil

100g (4oz) rice

1 orange, rind and juice

1 tablespoon vinegar

2 tablespoons white wine

280ml ($\frac{1}{2}$ pint) chicken stock

450g (1lb) cooked chicken, cubed

1 green pepper, very thinly sliced

70ml ($\frac{1}{8}$ pint) double cream

1 tablespoon mixed herbs

seasoning

Method

1. Melt butter and oil together in a frying pan. Fry the rice for 15 minutes approximately.

2. Add orange juice, vinegar, wine, chicken stock and chicken. Cook until rice is tender.

3. Add green pepper.

4. Mix together cream, herbs, orange peel and add to rice mixture.

5. Heat through but do not boil.

6. Garnish with sliced oranges.

Pork Parcels

4 pork chops

25g (1oz) butter

175g (6oz) mushrooms, sliced

1 small onion, chopped

1 tablespoon lemon juice

25g (1oz) wholemeal flour

seasoning

140ml ($\frac{1}{4}$ pint) natural yogurt

4 slices lemon

Oven temperature: 170°C/325°F/No. 3
Position in oven: Top
Time in oven: 1 hour, approximately
Serves **4**

Method

1. In a frying pan melt butter and brown pork chops on both sides.

2. Remove chops from pan. Add the mushrooms, onion and lemon juice. Sprinkle with flour and cook until thickened. Season.

3. Lightly butter 4 pieces of baking foil, each large enough to wrap a chop in.

4. Place 1 chop in each piece of foil, then divide mushroom mixture over the chops.

5. Spoon yogurt over the mushroom mixture and lay a lemon slice on top.

6. Close and seal the foil parcels and place on a baking sheet. Cook for 1 hour or until the pork chops are tender. Serve wrapped in parcels with potatoes and vegetables.

Creamed Veal with Mushrooms

4 veal escalopes
50g (2oz) flour
2 tablespoons paprika
salt and pepper
75g (3oz) butter
1 onion, finely chopped
1 clove garlic, crushed
4 rashers bacon, chopped
2 tablespoons wine
280ml ($\frac{1}{2}$ pint) chicken stock
225g (8oz) mushrooms, sliced
200g (7oz) tin tomatoes
1 teaspoon rosemary
25g (1oz) flaked almonds
140ml ($\frac{1}{4}$ pint) single cream

Oven temperature: 180°C/350°F/No. 4
Position in oven: Centre
Time in oven: 1$\frac{1}{2}$ hours
Serves **4**
Method
1. Beat veal escalopes between two sheets of dampened greaseproof paper until they are thin.
2. Coat with seasoned flour.
3. Melt butter. Fry the escalopes gently on each side. Keep hot.
4. Gently fry onion, garlic and bacon.
5. *To make sauce* — add remaining flour to pan, stir in wine, can tomatoes, stock and rosemary. Bring to boil.
6. Add mushrooms and almonds.
7. Place veal escalopes in casserole dish. Pour sauce over and cook for 1$\frac{1}{2}$ hours.
8. Stir in cream and serve garnished with mushroom and flaked almonds.

Nutty Pork Meatballs

450g (1lb) lean minced pork
2 carrots, grated
1 small onion, chopped
100g (4oz) fresh wholemeal breadcrumbs
25g (1oz) sultanas
50g (2oz) peanuts
1 tablespoon tabasco
1 egg, beaten
salt and pepper
1 teaspoon mixed herbs
50g (2oz) butter
50g (2oz) wholemeal flour
200ml ($\frac{1}{3}$ pint) milk
200g (7oz) can chopped tomatoes
100g (4oz) mushrooms, sliced
350g (12oz) wholemeal spaghetti

Oven temperature: 200°C/400°F/No. 6
Position in oven: Centre
Time in oven: 1$\frac{1}{2}$ hours
Serves **4-6**
Method
1. Place pork, carrots, onion, breadcrumbs and sultanas in a bowl, mix together.
2. Add peanuts, tabasco, egg and seasoning and combine all ingredients together.
3. Divide mixture into 16 and roll into balls and place in an ovenproof dish. Cover.
4. *To make sauce* — melt butter, blend in flour and gradually blend in milk and tomatoes. Bring to boil stirring all the time. Cook for 2-3 minutes, add mushrooms. Pour over meatballs and cook in oven.
5. Cook spaghetti in boiling salted water for approximately 12 minutes until tender.
6. Serve nutty pork meatballs on a bed of spaghetti.

Hungarian Beef

675g (1½lbs) stewing steak
50g (2oz) flour
salt and pepper
40g (1½oz) butter
2 medium onions
1 clove garlic, crushed
1 green pepper, chopped
1 tablespoon paprika
pinch nutmeg
3 tablespoons tomato purée
280ml (½ pint) beef stock
3 large tomatoes, skinned and sliced
100g (4oz) button mushrooms
bouquet garni
140ml (¼ pint) soured cream

Oven temperature:	170°C/325°F/No. 3
Position in oven:	Centre
Time in oven:	1½-2 hours or until meat is tender

Serves **4**
Method
1. Cut meat into 1 inch square cubes then coat with seasoned flour.
2. Fry onions, garlic and pepper lightly in butter, add meat, paprika and nutmeg and fry until golden brown.
3. Stir in tomato purée and remainder of flour.
4. Pour in stock, add sliced tomatoes, mushrooms and bouquet garni.
5. Cover and cook in oven for 1½–2 hours or until meat is tender.
6. Remove bouquet garni.
7. Spoon soured cream over goulash before serving. Serve on a bed of rice.

Lamb Pilaff

675g (1½lb) minced lamb
25g (1oz) butter
2 onions, finely chopped
50g (2oz) mixed nuts
50g (2oz) raisins
225g (8oz) brown rice
2 tablespoons tomato purée
1 teaspoon coriander
1 teaspoon cinnamon
100g (4oz) cooked peas
50g (2oz) Scottish cheddar cheese
140ml (¼ pint) natural yogurt
560ml (1 pint) lamb stock

Serves **4-6**
Method
1. Melt butter. Brown lamb, then drain fat.
2. Add onion and fry gently.
3. Stir in nuts, raisins, rice, tomato purée, spices and peas.
4. Add lamb stock. Bring to boil.
5. Lower heat, cover and simmer for 30 minutes or until rice is tender and stock absorbed.
6. Remove lid, add grated cheese and natural yogurt.
7. Mix well and serve.

Malayan Curry

50g (2oz) butter
4 chicken portions, skinned
2 large onions, chopped
25g (1oz) flour
2 tablespoons curry paste
560ml (1 pint) chicken stock
2 cloves
2 teaspoons ground ginger
2 teaspoons cinnamon
50g (2oz) flaked almonds
2 large bananas, chopped
140ml (¼ pint) single cream

Serves **4**
Method
1. Melt butter and gently brown chicken portions. Remove from pan and add chopped onions and cook until soft.
2. Stir in flour and cook for 1-2 minutes.
3. Add curry paste and gradually add in chicken stock.
4. Add all the other ingredients except the cream and return chicken portions to pan.
5. Simmer for 30-40 minutes or until chicken is tender.
6. Stir in cream and serve with boiled rice.

Pita Pockets

225g (8oz) cottage cheese
2 pineapple rings, chopped
100g (4oz) lean ham, cubed
25g (1oz) sultanas
$\frac{1}{4}$ cucumber, diced
2 tablespoons mayonnaise
1 tablespoon vinegar
seasoning
3 wholewheat pita bread
25g (1oz) butter
1 lettuce
cress to garnish

Method
1. In a large bowl, mix together cottage cheese, pineapple, ham, sultanas, cucumber, mayonnaise, vinegar and seasoning.
2. Cut each pita bread in half and butter the inside of each pocket. Line with lettuce leaves.
3. Evenly divide salad mixture among pockets. Serve.

Oriental Curried Rice

140ml ($\frac{1}{4}$ pint) natural yogurt
2 tablespoons mayonnaise
2 teaspoons curry powder
4 tablespoons lemon juice
seasoning
225g (8oz) brown rice, cooked, cooled
2 bananas, sliced
1 orange, cut into segments
75g (3oz) green grapes, halved and pipped
50g (2oz) walnut halves
1 red apple, cored and chopped

Method
1. In a bowl, mix together yogurt, mayonnaise, curry powder, lemon juice and seasoning.
2. Add rice, bananas, orange segments, grapes, walnuts and apples.
3. Toss the ingredients in the dressing until well coated.
4. Arrange in a serving dish.

Summer Pasta Salad

1 heaped tablespoon mayonnaise
1 tablespoon lemon juice
140ml ($\frac{1}{4}$ pint) natural yogurt
seasoning
75g (3oz) tin tuna fish, drained and flaked
150g (6oz) macaroni, cooked and drained
2 tomatoes, chopped
$\frac{1}{4}$ cucumber, diced
100g (4oz) Scottish cheddar cheese, cubed
4 sticks celery, chopped

Method
1. In a bowl, blend mayonnaise and lemon juice
into yogurt. Season.
2. Fold in remaining ingredients.
3. Serve on a bed of lettuce.

Crunchy Vegetable Salad

2 tablespoons, crunchy peanut butter
140ml ($\frac{1}{4}$ pint) natural yogurt
1 teaspoon freshly chopped parsley
seasoning
100g (4oz) Scottish cheddar cheese, cubed
100g (4oz) potatoes, cooked and diced
50g (2oz) sweetcorn
1 lettuce to serve

Method
1. In a bowl, blend the peanut butter into the
yogurt. Mix in the parsley and season.
2. Fold in the remaining ingredients into the
dressing.
3. Serve on a bed of lettuce.

Pear and Walnut Salad

3 large pears, peeled and halved

2 tablespoons lemon juice

1 lettuce, washed and shredded

140ml ($\frac{1}{4}$ pint) natural yogurt

225g (8oz) cottage cheese

50g (2oz) walnuts, chopped

garnish with lemon, lime, cucumber or cress as desired

Method

1. Dip pear halves in lemon juice then arrange on a bed of lettuce in a serving dish.

2. In a bowl combine yogurt with cottage cheese and walnuts.

3. Pile cottage cheese mixture onto pear halves.

4. Garnish as desired.

Honey Dew Salad

140ml ($\frac{1}{4}$ pint) double cream

1 tablespoon lemon juice

seasoning

1 honeydew melon

225g (8oz) cooked chicken, chopped

100g (4oz) black grapes, halved and pips removed

grapes to garnish

Method

1. In a large bowl blend cream, lemon juice and seasoning together.

2. Cut melon in half crossways and remove seeds. Scoop out flesh with a melon baller and chop any remaining flesh.

3. Fold melon, chicken and grapes into dressing.

4. Pile melon mixture back into melon halves.

Cheddar Bean Salad

225g (8oz) assorted dried beans (kidney, soya, haricot, pinto or black eye)

1 red apple, diced

225g (8oz) carrot, grated

140ml (¼ pint) natural yogurt

2 tablespoons lemon juice

3 tablespoons freshly chopped parsley

seasoning

150g (6oz) Scottish cheddar cheese, cubed

Method

1. Soak beans overnight in cold water.

2. Boil beans in fresh water for 20 minutes or until tender. Drain and allow to cool.

3. In a bowl, mix beans, apple, carrot, yogurt, lemon juice, 2 tablespoons parsley and seasoning.

4. Pile mixture into a serving dish.

5. Arrange cubes of cheese on top. Serve.

Orange Salad

140ml (¼ pint) single cream

2 tablespoons mayonnaise

100g (4oz) Scottish cheddar cheese, cubed

300g (11oz) can mandarin oranges, drained

225g (8oz) carrots, cut into inch long strips

1 lettuce to serve

Method

1. In a bowl blend cream and mayonnaise.

2. Add cheese, oranges and carrot and coat in dressing.

3. Serve on a bed of lettuce.

Haddock Lasagne

25g (1oz) butter	
225g (8oz) onion, chopped	
1 clove garlic, crushed	
1 green pepper, chopped	
50g (2oz) mushrooms, sliced	
1 bay leaf	
1 teaspoon mixed herbs	
400g (14oz) tin tomatoes	
1 tablespoon tomato purée	
2 fillets smoked haddock	
100g (4oz) tin prawns, optional	
225g (8oz) pre-cooked lasagne	
parsley to garnish	
40g (1½oz) butter	
40g (1½oz) flour	sauce
560ml (1 pint) milk	
100g (4oz) Scottish cheddar cheese, grated	

Oven temperature: 190°C/375°F/No. 5
Position in oven: Centre
Time in oven: 40-45 minutes
Serves **4**
Method
1. Melt butter and gently fry onion, garlic, pepper and mushrooms until soft.
2. Add bay leaf, herbs, tomatoes and tomato purée and bring to the boil.
3. Add prawns and haddock and simmer for 5 minutes.
4. Make white sauce (page 86).
5. Add half the cheese and stir until it melts, season.
6. Put alternate layers of lasagne, fish mixture and sauce in an ovenproof casserole, beginning with lasagne and finishing with white sauce.
7. Sprinkle with remaining cheese.
8. Garnish with parsley. Serve with a crisp green salad and french bread.

Cheesy Cod Pie

25g (1oz) butter	
25g (1oz) plain flour	
280ml (½ pint) milk	sauce
pinch mustard	
seasoning	
100g (4oz) Scottish cheddar cheese, grated	
450g (1lb) cod, cooked and flaked	
225g (8oz) cauliflower florets, cooked	
2 (size 3) eggs, hard boiled	

900g (2 lb) potatoes, boiled	
25g (1oz) butter	
4 tablespoons milk	

Oven temperature: 180°C/350°F/No. 4
Position in oven: Top
Time in oven: 20-25 minutes
Serves **4**
Method
1. *Sauce* — in a pan melt butter then add flour and cook for 1 minute. Gradually blend in milk and cook until sauce thickens.
2. Add mustard, seasoning and 75g (3oz) cheese to the sauce.
3. Stir in cod, cauliflower and chopped boiled eggs.
4. Pour mixture into buttered individual dishes or one large ovenproof casserole.
5. Mash potatoes with butter and milk.
6. Pipe potato around the edge of the casserole dish. Sprinkle with remaining cheese.
7. Bake. Serve immediately, garnished with parsley.

Haddock Souffle

225g (8oz) smoked haddock	
280ml (½ pint) milk	
25g (1oz) butter	
25g (1oz) wholemeal flour	
100g (4oz) Scottish cheddar cheese, grated	
juice and rind of 1 lemon	
salt and pepper	
1 teaspoon rosemary	
2 (size 2) eggs, separated	

Oven temperature: 190°C/375°F/No. 5
Position in oven: Centre
Time in oven: 45-50 minutes
Serves **4**
Method
1. Cook fish in milk for 10-12 minutes or until fish flakes easily.
2. Remove from pan. Discard skin and bones. Reserve cooking liquid.
3. Flake fish.
4. Melt butter, add flour and cook for 1 minute. Gradually add reserved cooking liquid and cook 1-2 minutes to make a thick smooth sauce.
5. Allow to cool.
6. Stir in fish, cheese, lemon and seasoning.
7. Beat in egg yolks.
8. Whisk egg white until it holds soft peaks. Fold into fish mixture.
9. Place in greased 700ml (1¼ pint) dish and bake for 45-50 minutes or until set.

Sole in Coriander Cream

75g (3oz) butter

4 fillets lemon sole

juice and rind of 1 orange

2 level teaspoons ground coriander

140ml ($\frac{1}{4}$ pint) double cream

seasoning

garnish with slices of orange.

Method

1. Melt butter in frying pan and gently fry sole with orange juice added.

2. When sole is cooked, remove from pan and keep warm in a serving dish.

3. Add orange rind, coriander and cream to butter in which sole has been cooked. Bring to boil.

4. Boil for 1-2 minutes until all ingredients are mixed and begin to thicken.

5. Season. Remove from heat and pour over sole.

6. Serve garnished with orange slices.

Spicy Prawn Bake

50g (2oz) butter

1 clove garlic, crushed

2 syboes, chopped

225g (8oz) smoked haddock, cubed

1 banana, sliced

2 teaspoons curry powder

15g ($\frac{1}{2}$oz) dessicated coconut

25g (1oz) plain flour

140ml ($\frac{1}{4}$ pint) milk

225g (8oz) prawns

25g (1oz) Scottish cheddar cheese, grated ⎤

15g ($\frac{1}{2}$oz) dessicated coconut ⎦ topping

Method

1. In a frying pan, melt butter. Add garlic, syboes, smoked haddock, banana and curry powder together. Sauté gently until fish is cooked.

2. Stir in coconut and plain flour and cook for 1 minute.

3. Stir milk in gradually then add prawns. Cook until mixture thickens.

4. Place mixture into a fireproof serving dish. Sprinkle with cheese and coconut. Place under a hot grill to brown.

5. Serve hot with boiled rice.

Salmon Flan

150g (6oz) wholemeal flour ⎤

pinch salt

$\frac{1}{2}$ teaspoon baking powder ⎥ wholemeal pastry

75g (3oz) butter

3-4 tablespoons milk ⎦

25g (1oz) butter ⎤

1 small onion, chopped

$\frac{1}{2}$ small green pepper, chopped

200g (7oz) tin salmon, drained and flaked ⎥ filling

seasoning

140ml ($\frac{1}{4}$ pint) single cream

2 (size 3) eggs, lightly beaten

50g (2oz) Scottish cheddar cheese ⎦

parsley to garnish

Oven temperature:	200°C/400°F/No. 6
Position in oven:	Top
Time in oven:	35-40 minutes

Serves **6-8**

Method

1. *Pastry* — sieve dry ingredients together. Rub butter into flour.

2. Add milk gradually to form a soft dough.

3. Refrigerate for 10 minutes then roll out and line a 20cm (8 inch) flan ring. Bake blind at 180°C/350°F/No. 4 for 15 minutes.

4. *Filling* — melt butter in a frying pan. Add the onion and cook until soft. Stir in the green pepper, salmon and seasoning. Cook for 2 minutes.

5. Mix cream, eggs and cheese together. Add onions and peppers to egg mixture then pour into flan case.

6. Bake until the filling is firm and golden brown. Serve hot or cold.

Marshmallow Cheesecake

150g (6oz) wholemeal biscuits	} base
75g (3oz) butter, melted	
225g (8oz) smooth cottage cheese	
2 tablespoons lemon juice	
2 tablespoons caster sugar	
1 teaspoon vanilla essence	
$\frac{1}{2}$ teaspoon almond essence	} filling
280ml ($\frac{1}{2}$ pint) double cream, whipped	
225g (8oz) marshmallows (chop 100g (4oz))	
50g (2oz) chocolate, melted	

Method
1. *Base* — mix biscuits with butter. Press biscuit mixture into the base of a 20cm (8 inch) loose bottomed cake tin.
2. *Filling* — mix together cottage cheese, lemon juice, caster sugar, vanilla essence and almond essence until smooth and well blended.
3. Fold in cream lightly then add chopped marshmallows.

4. Spread mixture carefully over the base.
5. Decorate with whole marshmallows drizzled with melted chocolate.

Banana Honey Cheesecake

150g (6oz) ginger nut biscuits, crushed	} base
75g (3oz) butter, melted	
225g (8oz) smooth cottage cheese	
140ml ($\frac{1}{4}$ pint) natural yogurt	
2 bananas	
4 tablespoons lemon juice	
2 tablespoons clear honey	} filling
50g (2oz) hazelnuts, chopped	
15g ($\frac{1}{2}$oz) galatine	
4 tablespoons water	
whipped cream and hazelnuts	decoration

Method
1. *Base* — add biscuits to butter and press into a 20cm (8 inch) loose bottomed cake tin. Chill.
2. Place cottage cheese and yogurt in a bowl and beat until fluffy.

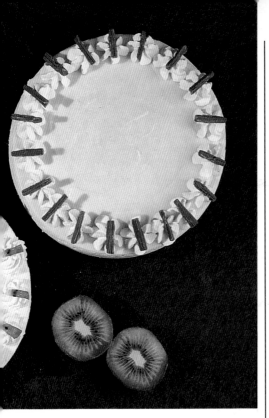

2. *Filling* — blend cottage cheese until smooth.
3. Add caster sugar and peach.
4. Gently fold in cream.
5. Spoon the mixture over the base and chill until firm.
6. Decorate with reserved cream, peach and kiwi fruit slices.

Butterscotch Cheesecake

100g (4oz) oatmeal biscuits, crushed	base
40g (1½oz) butter	
2 tablespoons cornflour	filling
280ml (½ pint) milk	
50g (2oz) butter	
150g (6oz) light soft brown sugar	
3 teaspoons vanilla essence	
150g (6oz) smooth cottage cheese	
280ml (½ pint) double cream, lightly whipped, reserve approximately 70ml (⅛ pint) cream for decoration	

Serves **4-6**
Method
1. *Base* — melt butter, add biscuit crumbs and press into a 15cm (6 inch) loose bottomed cake tin. Chill.
2. *Filling* — blend the cornflour with a little of the milk.
3. Place the rest of the milk, butter and sugar in a saucepan and heat gently until the sugar is dissolved.
4. Pour milk mixture over cornflour stirring well then return mixture to pan and bring to boil stirring constantly. Cook for 3-4 minutes then add vanilla essence. Allow to cool.
5. Beat cottage cheese until smooth, add butterscotch sauce and mix well.
6. Gently mix in lightly whipped cream and spoon the mixture over the base and chill until firm.
7. Decorate with cream and chocolate flake.

3. Peel and mash bananas with lemon juice. Add to cheese mixture with honey and mix well.
4. Fold in chopped hazelnuts.
5. Dissolve gelatine in water and then add to cheese mixture.
6. Pour mixture over biscuit base and smooth. Chill for at least 2 hours.
7. Decorate with cream and hazelnuts.

Peach and Kiwi Cheesecake

100g (4oz) oatmeal biscuits, crushed	base
40g (1½oz) butter	
1 peach, chopped	filling
50g (2oz) caster sugar	
150g (6oz) smooth cottage cheese	
280ml (½ pint) double cream, lightly whipped reserve approximately 70ml (⅛ pint) cream for decoration	

Method
1. *Base* — melt butter, add biscuit crumbs and press into a 15-16cm (6 inch) loose bottomed cake tin. Chill.

Pavlova with Kiwi Fruit and Strawberries

3 (size 3) egg whites
pinch salt
250g (9oz) caster sugar
1 teaspoon vanilla essence
1 teaspoon vinegar
280ml ($\frac{1}{2}$ pint) double cream
Kiwi fruit and strawberries to decorate

Oven temperature: 140°C/275°F/No. 1
Position in oven: Centre
Time in oven: 1 hour approximately
Serves **8**

Method
1. Draw a 23cm (9 inch) circle on non-stick baking parchment and place on a baking sheet.
2. Whisk the egg whites with the salt until very stiff, then gradually whisk in the sugar. With last lot of sugar, mix in vanilla essence and vinegar. Beat until it forms stiff peaks again.
3. Spread the meringue over the circle and bake until firm.
4. Leave to cool then carefully remove the paper and place the pavlova on a serving dish.
5. Whip the cream until stiff then pile onto meringue and decorate with the fruit.

Raspberry Brûlée

225g (8oz) raspberries
140ml (¼ pint) double cream, chilled
40g (1½oz) demerara sugar

Serves **4**
Method
1. Place raspberries in the base of four individual ovenproof dishes or one large dish.
2. Lightly whip cream and spread over raspberries.
3. Cover thickly with sugar and cook under a pre-heated grill until sugar melts.
4. Serve hot or cold.

Raspberry Drambuie Creams

225g (8oz) raspberries
140ml (¼ pint) double cream
140ml (¼ pint) natural yogurt
1 tablespoon caster sugar
2 tablespoons Drambuie
1 tablespoon pinhead oatmeal
1 tablespoon demerara sugar

Serves **4**
Method
1. Reserve 4 raspberries for decoration.
2. Place raspberries into individual stemmed glasses.
3. Whip cream, yogurt, caster sugar, and Drambuie together until stiff.
4. Spoon the cream over the raspberries.
5. Mix oatmeal and demerara sugar together. Sprinkle on top of the cream and top with a raspberry. Chill before serving.

Honey Pots

grated rind and juice of 1 orange	
3 tablespoons clear honey	
2 tablespoons brandy	
280ml (½ pint) double cream	
1 orange cut into segments	} *to serve*
few toasted flaked almonds	

Method
1. Mix rind and juice of orange with honey and brandy in a bowl and leave for 15 minutes.
2. Add cream and whip until stiff.
3. Pile mixture into individual glasses or pots.
4. Chill then serve with segments of fresh orange and toasted flaked almonds.

Plum Soufflé

340g (¾lb) stewed plums or 450g (1lb) jar plums, drained, stoned and puréed

3 (size 3) eggs separated

50g (2oz) caster sugar

140ml (¼ pint) natural yogurt

½ teaspoon almond essence

15g (½oz) gelatine

3 tablespoons water

140ml (¼ pint) double cream, whipped

flaked almonds and whipped cream to decorate

Method

1. Whisk plum purée, egg yolks, caster sugar, almond essence and natural yogurt together until creamy.

2. Dissolve gelatine in water and add to plum mixture.

3. Fold in cream and whisked egg whites. Pour into an 850ml (1½ pint) prepared soufflé dish and chill until set. Decorate with whipped cream and almonds.

Pear Condé

50g (2oz) pudding rice

50g (2oz) sugar

560ml (1 pint) milk

little butter

140ml (¼ pint) pear juice

3 tablespoons raspberry jam

1 teaspoon cornflour

4 pear halves

Method

1. Make baked rice (see Step by Step Cookery page 91) and allow to cool.

2. Make syrup by blending cornflour, pear juice and jam. Bring syrup to the boil and cook for 2 minutes. Strain and cool.

3. Divide rice into 4 individual dishes. Arrange pear halves cut side down on rice. Pour over syrup.

Brandied Peaches

140ml (¼ pint) double cream

1-2 tablespoons brandy

2 fresh peaches, stoned and cubed

4 scoops dairy ice cream

chocolate to decorate

Serves **4**

Method

1. Lightly whisk cream and brandy together.
2. Divide peach cubes amongst 4 stemmed glasses.
3. Top with ice cream and pour over brandy cream. Decorate with chocolate.

Hot Fudge Sauce

50g (2oz) butter

50g (2oz) soft brown sugar

2 tablespoons golden syrup

200g (7oz) tin condensed milk

Method

1. Place butter, sugar and syrup in a double saucepan and heat gently until sugar has melted.
2. Add condensed milk and cook for a further 2-3 minutes stirring all the time. Serve hot or cold with ice cream.

Strawberry Skyscraper

1 portion hot fudge sauce

225g (8oz) strawberries, sliced

2 bananas, sliced

4-8 scoops dairy ice cream

140ml (¼ pint) double cream, whipped

Serves **4**

Method

1. In tall glasses, arrange layers of strawberries, bananas, ice cream and fudge sauce.
2. Serve topped with cream and sliced strawberry.

Sunburst

140ml (¼ pint) orange juice

2 level teaspoons arrowroot

sugar to sweeten

1 kiwi fruit, halved and sliced

1 orange, cut into segments

1 scoop dairy ice cream

Serves **1**

Method

1. In a small saucepan, blend arrowroot with orange juice. Heat gently stirring continuously until liquid thickens. Cool.
2. Arrange orange and kiwi slices in a sunburst. Place ice cream in the middle and top with orange sauce.

Rocky Road Bars

100g (4oz) digestive biscuits, crushed	base
65g (2½oz) butter, melted	
100g (4oz) butter	filling
100g (4oz) soft brown sugar	
140ml (¼ pint) milk	
75g (3oz) coconut	
100g (4oz) maraschino cherries, drained and chopped	
100g (4oz) walnuts, chopped	
100g (4oz) marshmallows, chopped	
100g (4oz) digestive biscuits, crushed	
100g (4oz) plain chocolate	topping
25g (1oz) butter	

Method
1. Line a swiss roll tin with cling film.
2. *Base* — mix biscuits and butter together and press into base of tin.
3. In a saucepan heat butter, sugar and milk together. Bring mixture to the boil and boil for 3 minutes.
4. Remove from heat and stir in coconut, cherries, walnuts, marshmallows and biscuits.
5. Spread over the biscuit base.
6. Melt butter and chocolate together. Beat well until shiny and pour over filling. Cool to set.
7. Keep covered in the refrigerator.
Cut into 36 bars.

Nanaimo Bars

75g (3oz) butter	base
50g (2oz) granulated sugar	
3 tablespoons drinking chocolate	
1 egg (size 3)	
200g (7oz) digestive biscuits	
40g (1½oz) coconut	
50g (2oz) walnuts, chopped	
75g (3oz) butter	filling
3 tablespoons milk	
2 tablespoons custard powder	
275g (10oz) icing sugar, sieved	
100g (4oz) plain chocolate	topping
50g (2oz) butter	

Method
1. *Base* — over a low heat melt the butter, sugar and drinking chocolate.
2. Add beaten egg and stir to cook and thicken.
3. Remove from heat. Stir in biscuit crumbs, coconut and walnuts.
4. Press into a swiss roll tin.
5. *Filling* — cream butter, milk, custard powder and icing sugar together. Beat until light, then spread over base.
6. *Topping* — melt chocolate and butter over a low heat. Cool. When cool but still runny spread over filling. Chill and store in refrigerator.
Cut into 36 bars.

Orange Chocolate Tiffin

225g (8oz) digestive biscuits, crushed
50g (2oz) sultanas
100g (4oz) butter
3 level tablespoons syrup
25g (1oz) drinking chocolate
150g (6oz) cooking chocolate
juice and rind of $\frac{1}{2}$ orange

Method
1. Line a swiss roll tin with clingfilm.
2. Melt butter and syrup in a pan. Add sultanas, drinking chocolate and biscuits. Mix well.
3. Place mixture in a prepared tin. Press well, leave until cold.
4. Melt chocolate with juice and rind of orange in a bowl over boiling water and pour over mixture spreading evenly.
5. When set, pull out tiffin with clingfilm and cut into required size.

Nutty Wholewheat Shortbread

340g (12oz) wholemeal flour
pinch salt
$\frac{1}{2}$ teaspoon baking powder
50g (2oz) walnuts, finely chopped
225g (8oz) butter
75g (3oz) granulated sugar

Oven temperature: 180°C/350°F/No. 4
Position in oven: Centre
Time in oven: 50-60 minutes
Makes: 2 × 15cm (6 inch) rounds
Method
1. Sieve salt and baking powder into flour. Stir in walnuts.
2. Cream butter and sugar well.
3. Gradually work the flour into creamed mixture and knead until smooth.
4. Form mixture into two rounds.
5. Prick all over with a fork. Bake.
6. Cut into required size of pieces when hot and sprinkle with caster sugar. Cool on a wire rack.

Wholemeal Chocolate Cake

100g (4oz) wholemeal flour	⎫
50g (2oz) drinking chocolate	⎬ mix
2 teaspoons baking powder	⎭
150g (6oz) butter	
100g (4oz) dark brown sugar	
2 tablespoons honey	
3 (size 3) eggs	
3 tablespoons milk	
140ml (¼ pint) double cream	⎫
1 tablespoon lemon juice	⎬ filling
1 large banana, mashed	⎭
75g (3oz) plain or milk chocolate – topping	

Oven temperature: 180°C/350°F/No. 4
Position in oven: Centre
Time in oven: 35 minutes
Method
1. Grease and line two 18cm (7 inch) cake tins.
2. Cream butter, sugar and honey then beat in eggs one at a time.
3. Fold in flour mixture then blend in milk.
4. Divide mixture between the two tins.
5. Bake until well risen and firm to touch. Cool.
6. Whip cream and fold through banana and lemon juice. Sandwich cake together with cream.
7. Melt chocolate and smooth over top of cake. Allow chocolate to set before serving.

Peanut Butter Cookies

25g (1oz) self raising flour
25g (1oz) pinhead oatmeal
100g (4oz) wholemeal flour
2 rounded teaspoons baking powder
75g (3oz) peanut butter
75g (3oz) butter
1 tablespoon golden syrup
50g (2oz) dark soft brown sugar

Oven temperature: 180°C/350°F/No. 4
Position in oven: Centre
Time in oven: 15 minutes
Makes: 20-25
Method
1. Melt butter, syrup and sugar.
2. Add peanut butter. Mix thoroughly.
3. Sieve flour and baking powder. Add oatmeal.
4. Stir dry ingredients into melted butter and mix thoroughly.

5. Roll into balls and place on a lightly greased baking tray.
6. Bake.
7. Allow to cool.

Orchard Scones

100g (4oz) wholemeal flour	
100g (4oz) plain flour	
½ teaspoon salt	
2 teaspoons baking powder	
50g (2oz) butter	
50g (2oz) caster sugar	
1 medium sized cooking apple, peeled, cored and grated	
4 tablespoons milk	
milk and 1-2 tablespoons demerara sugar	⎱ glaze

Oven temperature: 200°C/400°F/No. 6
Position in oven: Top
Time in oven: 25-30 minutes
Makes: 8 scones
Method
1. Sieve plain flour, salt and baking powder together into a bowl, and mix in wholemeal flour.
2. Rub in the butter. Add the sugar and grated apple.
3. Gradually add the milk to make a soft but not sticky dough.
4. Turn mixture out onto a floured board and knead lightly.
5. Roll out into a 20cm (8 inch) circle and place on a floured baking sheet.
6. Score into 8 pieces. Brush the top with milk and sprinkle with sugar.
7. Bake until golden brown and serve warm with butter.

Banana Zap

560ml (1 pint) milk

1 banana

225g (8oz) lychees, fresh or tinned

Serves **2-4**

Method

1. Place milk, banana and lychees in liquidiser. Liquidise for 1 minute.

2. Sieve. Chill.

3. Serve in a tall glass with crushed ice.

Mock Cappuccino

280ml (½ pint) milk

280ml (½ pint) boiling water

2 teaspoons instant coffee

To decorate: whipped cream and grated chocolate

Serves **2-4**

Method

1. Heat milk and coffee powder in a saucepan.

2. Add boiling water. Stir.

3. Serve hot in a cup and top with whipped cream. Sprinkle with grated chocolate.

Ming Zing

560ml (1 pint) milk

100g (4oz) mangoes, fresh or tinned

100g (4oz) lychees, fresh or tinned

Serves **2-4**

Method

1. Place milk, mangoes and lychees in liquidiser. Liquidise for 1 minute.

2. Sieve. Chill.

3. Serve in a tall glass with crushed ice.

Pineapple Sunburst

280ml (½ pint) milk

100g (4oz) crushed pineapple

140ml (¼ pint) carton pineapple yogurt

1 tablespoon castor sugar

3 tablespoons rum

Serves **2-4**

Method

1. Whisk together milk, crushed pineapple, yogurt, sugar and rum.

2. Sieve. Chill.

3. Serve in a tall glass with crushed ice.

One of the delightful aspects about travelling abroad
is to taste the traditional dishes of the country.
Generally these are derived from foods which are abundant in the area.

With the co-operation of Home Economists from ten different countries
in similar organisations to The Scottish Milk Marketing Board,
we present to you the following recipes:

——FROM AUSTRALIA——
Peach Melba
Sent by Ann Merrett, Australian Dairy Corporation

——FROM CANADA——
Turkey Pot Pie
Sent by Darlene Laurendeau, Milk Marketing Board of Ontario

——FROM DENMARK——
Enebaergryde – Juniper Berry Casserole
Sent by Jytte Nipper, Danish Dairy Board

——FROM FRANCE——
Croquettes de Camembert – Camembert Croquettes
Sent by Laetitia Crahay
Centre Interprofessionnel De Documentation et D'information Laitières

——FROM GERMANY——
Blutwurst mit Äpfeln – Black Pudding with Apple
Sent by Messrs Fuhrmann and Vellrath
Centrale Marketing Gisellschaft der Deutschen Agrarwirtschaft

——FROM HOLLAND——
Dutch Vermicelli Soup with Cheesy Meatballs
Sent by Valerie Kimmell of the Dutch Dairy Bureau

——FROM NEW ZEALAND——
Groper Mushroom and Cheese
Sent by Jennifer Leman, New Zealand Milk Board

——FROM SPAIN——
Leche Frita – Fried Milk
Sent by Maria José Sevile at the Spanish Embassy Commercial Office

——FROM THE IRISH REPUBLIC——
Fillet Steak Gaelic Style
Sent by Anne M Byrne and Denise Sweeney, National Dairy Council

——FROM U.S.A.——
Bavarian Pumpkin Cheesecake
Sent by Elizabeth P Graham, Washington Dairy Products Commission
via Mary Rowland, Washington State Dairy Council.

I would like to express my grateful thanks to all the people named above
whose recipes appear on the following pages.

Peach Melba

6 small pastry cases	
6 halves fresh or canned peaches	
6 scoops ice cream	
140ml (¼ pint) double cream, whipped	
1 tablespoon chopped nuts	
140ml (¼ pint) peach juice	⎫
3 tablespoons raspberries, crushed or raspberry jam	⎬ sauce
1 teaspoon cornflour or arrowroot	⎭

Method
1. Make syrup by blending cornflour, juice and fruit together, crushing the raspberries well. Bring syrup to the boil and cook for 2 minutes. Strain and cool.
2. Place half peach in pastry case, hollow side up. Put a scoop of ice cream into the peach and cover with melba sauce.
3. Decorate with cream and nuts.
This recipe was created by Escoffier, the famous French chef for the opera singer Dame Nellie Melba who obviously had a sweet tooth.

CANADA—

Turkey Pot Pie with Herbed Dumpling Crust

65g (2½oz) butter	
225g (½lb) mushrooms, quartered	
50g (2oz) flour	
280ml (½ pint) chicken stock	
560ml (1 pint) milk	
½ teaspoon dried thyme	
¼ teaspoon tabasco sauce	
450g (1lb) diced cooked turkey (or chicken or ham)	
50g (2oz) diced pimento	
225g (½lb) cooked vegetables	
225g (½lb) flour	
2 teaspoons baking powder	
1 tablespoon chopped fresh parsley	
1 tablespoon chopped fresh dill (or ½ teaspoon dried dill)	herb dumpling crust
¼ teaspoon salt	
65g (2½oz) butter	
140ml (¼ pint) milk, cold (plus 2 tablespoons)	

Preparation time: 30 minutes
Cooking time: 30 minutes
Serves **6**
Method
1. Melt butter in large saucepan. Add mushrooms. Cook a few minutes. Sprinkle with flour. Cook 5 minutes, do not brown. Whisk in stock and milk. Bring to boil. Reduce heat. Add seasonings and salt and pepper to taste. Simmer gently, stirring occasionally, 10 minutes.
2. Add turkey, pimento and vegetables to sauce.
3. Preheat oven to 200°C/400°F/Gas 6. Butter a 3 litre/5 pint casserole dish.
4. Prepare dumpling crust by combining flour with baking powder, parsley, dill and salt. Cut in butter until it is in tiny bits. Sprinkle mixture with milk. Gather together to form a dough.
5. Roll dough on floured surface to fit the top of the casserole.
6. Spoon turkey mixture into casserole. Place dough directly on top of turkey. Cut steam slits in dough. Brush with remaining 2 tablespoons milk.
7. Bake 30-35 minutes.

Enebaergryde
Juniper Stew with Baked Potato Mash

1kg (2lb) pork in cubes
50g (2oz) butter
6 juniper berries
$\frac{1}{2}$ teaspoon dried rosemary
$\frac{1}{4}$ litre (280ml) whipping cream
2 tablespoons sour cream
1 teaspoon seasalt
freshly milled pepper
gravy browning
thickening, if required

750g (1½lb) potatoes	
50g (2oz) butter	
1 tablespoon whipping cream	
2 eggs	potato mash
1 tablespoon chopped hazelnuts (optional)	
1 teaspoon seasalt	
freshly ground pepper	

Oven temperature: 225°C/425°F/No. 7
Position in oven: Middle
Time in oven: 25 minutes
Serves **4**

Method
1. Cut the pork into thin strips. Melt the butter in pan, add pork and brown well.
2. Crush juniper berries and rosemary and add to the meat. Add whipping cream, sour cream, salt and pepper.
3. Cover the pot with a lid and gently simmer for approximately 60 minutes. Season and add gravy browning. The stew may be thickened, if necessary.
4. *Potato mash* – peel the potatoes and cut into small pieces.
5. Boil for approximately 20 minutes till well done. Pour off water and steam.
6. Mash the potatoes and stir in butter and whipping cream. Whip egg yolks in one at a time. Add hazelnuts and season with salt and pepper.
7. Whip egg whites and carefully add to the potato mash.
8. Pour into 4-6 buttered portion dishes and bake them in the middle of the oven. Serve immediately.
Tip – the potato mash may also be baked in a buttered soufflé form. Baking time approximately 35 minutes at 200°C.
The juniper stew and the baked potato mash may be made some hours in advance and be ready for heating and baking.

FRANCE—
Camembert Croquettes

A delicious savoury for cocktail time.

125g (5oz) camembert or Lothian cheese
75g (3oz) smooth cottage cheese
25g (1oz) butter, softened
15g (½oz) cornflour
15g (½oz) flour
1 (size 3) egg yolk
½ teaspoon mustard powder
pinch cayenne pepper
seasoning
50g (2oz) plain flour
1-2 (size 3) eggs, beaten
oil for frying

Serves **6**

Method
1. Remove skin from camembert. Place in a bowl with cottage cheese, butter, cornflour and flour.
2. Place over a pan of hot water and blend until smooth.
3. Remove from the heat and stir in egg yolk, mustard powder, cayenne pepper and seasoning. Leave to cool for at least 2 hours.
4. Take a heaped teaspoon of cheese mixture and shape into a croquette. Dip in flour, egg and breadcrumbs twice.
5. Cook croquettes in hot oil until golden brown. Drain and serve hot.

Blutwurst mit Äpfeln
Black Pudding with Apples

500g (1lb) black pudding
500g (1lb) cooking apples
60g (2½oz) butter
a little ground cinnamon
seasoning

Serves **4**

Method
1. Cut the apples into large pieces, cook in
butter until the apple is brown, add a pinch of
salt and dust with cinnamon, remove from pan.
2. Cut round the edges of the black pudding and
cook in butter until it is sizzling.
3. Add the apple pieces and stir for a further five
minutes. Serve immediately.

HOLLAND—
Dutch Vermicelli Soup with Cheesy Meatballs

25g (1oz) unsalted butter	
1 onion, chopped	
25g (1oz) flour	
1½ litres (3 pints) chicken stock	
1 teaspoon ground mace	
black pepper	
50g (2oz) fine vermicelli pasta	
225g (8oz) minced beef	⎫
1 egg	⎪
75g (3oz) Dutch Edam cheese, grated	⎬ meatballs
salt and black pepper	⎪
¼ teaspoon ground nutmeg	⎭

Serves **6**

Method
1. Melt the butter in a large saucepan and sauté the onion.
2. Stir in the flour and cook for a further minute.
3. Add the chicken stock, mace and seasonings. Bring to the boil.
4. Mix all the ingredients for the meatballs together and using a little flour, roll into small balls.
5. Add the meat balls and vermicelli to the soup, cover the pan and simmer gently for 15 minutes.

Fillet Steak Gaelic Style

50g (2oz) butter

4 fillet steaks (4-6oz each)

2 tablespoons shallots, chopped

100g (4oz) button mushrooms, cleaned and cut into quarters

250ml ($\frac{1}{2}$ pint) cream

dash Irish whiskey

freshly ground black pepper and salt

Method

1. Melt butter in a large heavy based frying pan, add steaks and cook quickly on both sides to seal. Cook for a further 1-2 minutes according to individual taste.
2. Remove steaks from pan and keep hot.
3. Add shallots, cook until tender, add mushrooms and cook until lightly browned.
4. Stir in cream and whiskey to pan, cook over a low heat until cream reduces and sauces thicken. Season to taste.
5. Pour sauce over steaks and garnish.

Groper Mushrooms and Cheese

4 fillets groper (or any other white fish e.g. cod, haddock, sole, whiting)
450ml (¾ pint) milk
1 clove garlic
2 tablespoons flour
50g (2oz) butter
50g (2oz) grated cheese (cheddar, gruyere or edam)
50g (2oz) sliced mushrooms
2 tomatoes skinned and quartered
1 bay leaf
salt and pepper

Serves **4**

Method
1. Put milk, bayleaf, crushed garlic and seasoning in a pan and heat to boiling point but do not boil.
2. Place fish in pan and poach in the milk mixture gently until cooked (about 4-8 minutes).
3. Place fish on a serving plate and keep hot.
4. Mix butter and flour together, strain milk and mix all together in a pot and bring to boil, stirring.
5. Add mushrooms and cheese and cook for 2-3 minutes.
6. Pour over fish and decorate with mushrooms and tomatoes.

SPAIN—
Leche Frita Fried Milk

75g (3oz) butter
100g (4oz) plain flour
125g (5oz) caster sugar
140ml ($\frac{1}{4}$ pint) milk
$\frac{1}{2}$ teaspoon vanilla essence
2 egg yolks
1 egg, beaten
225g (8oz) breadcrumbs
oil for frying
icing sugar to decorate

Method
1. Melt the butter in a saucepan. Add 75g (3oz) flour and cook for 2 minutes. Add the sugar and mix well.
2. Gradually add the milk to the flour mixture and bring to the boil. Remove from heat.
3. Stir in the egg yolks one at a time. Add vanilla essence. This mixture should have a paste-like consistency.
For best results pour into a chilled tin. Leave to cool then take a teaspoon of mixture and roll into balls. Dip each piece into remaining flour, beaten eggs and breadcrumbs. Fry in hot oil until golden brown. Serve dusted with icing sugar.

Bavarian Pumpkin Cheesecake

340g (12oz) pumpkin purée	
140ml (¼ pint) sour cream	
2 egg yolks	
½ teaspoon ground ginger	bottom layer
½ teaspoon ground nutmeg	
⅛ teaspoon ground cloves	
100g (4oz) sugar	
4 egg whites	
150g (6oz) ginger snap crumbs	middle layer
50g (2oz) melted butter	
2 egg yolks	
140ml (¼ pint) sour cream	
40g (1½oz) sugar	top layer
1 tablespoon flour	
½ teaspoon vanilla essence	
225g (8oz) cream cheese	
140ml (¼ pint) double cream for decoration	

Serves **10-12**

Method

Bottom layer

1. Mix pumpkin purée, sour cream, yolks, spices and ⅓ sugar.

2. Beat egg whites and sugar. Fold into pumpkin mixture.

3. Pour into greased loose bottomed 23cm (9 inch) tin.

Middle layer

1. Mix gingersnap crumbs and butter, sprinkle over lower layer.

Top layer

1. Beat yolks until pale, mix in sour cream, sugar, flour and vanilla essence.

2. Beat in cream cheese until smooth and carefully pour over crumbs.

3. Bake at 160°C/325°F for 55-60 minutes or until set.

4. Chill and decorate with rosettes of double cream and a little freshly grated nutmeg if desired.

Cooking with a microwave oven

Microwave cookery is very different in many ways from cooking with a conventional cooker. A microwave oven will thaw frozen food, cook fresh food and reheat cooked food very efficiently.

The directions which you receive with your microwave oven should give you an idea of how it works and what you can and cannot do with microwaves.

The following recipes have been tried and tested on a 700 watt model. If you have a 650 watt or a 500 watt oven then add 10 and 15 seconds longer for each minute, respectively.

Where high power is referred to — this means 100% power.

Where medium power is referred to — this means 60% power.

Where low power is referred to — this means 30% power.

Food is cooked very rapidly by microwaves therefore it is always safer to undercook and return again to the oven after standing time, if necessary. When food is removed from the microwave oven it continues cooking from the heat generated within itself, this is called standing time and is an important part to complete cooking.

It is useful to make notes on a recipe, if it takes longer or shorter than suggested, this can alter for various reasons and you can improve your cooking results by careful monitoring.

You will discover the many dishes which you enjoy from your microwave oven, the time, electricity and washing up that you save, all pluses in todays lifestyle. Enjoy your microwave cooking.

Porridge

25g (1oz) porridge oats

420ml (¾ pint) milk

Salt

Serves **1**

Method

1. Blend porridge oats and milk in a bowl.

2. Add a little salt.

3. Do not cover.

4. Microwave on high for 4-5 minutes, stirring after 2 minutes.

5. Stir and serve.

Custard

280ml (½ pint) milk

1 tablespoon sugar

1 tablespoon custard powder

few drops vanilla essence

Method

1. Place custard powder, sugar, vanilla essence in a measuring jug.

2. With 1 tablespoon milk, mix ingredients together to form a smooth paste.

3. Gradually add the rest of the milk. Microwave on high for 3 minutes, stirring every minute.

Basic White Sauce

25g (1oz) butter

25g (1oz) flour

280ml (½ pint) milk

seasoning

Method

1. Place butter in a glass bowl. Microwave on high for 30 seconds.

2. Stir in flour, then gradually add milk. Microwave on high for 4 minutes, stirring every minute.

3. Season and serve.

Cheese and Tomato Soup

40g (1½oz) butter
1 medium onion, finely chopped
40g (1½oz) plain flour
2 teaspoons tomato purée
140ml (¼ pint) chicken stock, warmed
560ml (1 pint) milk, warmed
6 tomatoes, skinned and chopped
150g (6oz) Scottish cheddar cheese, grated
seasoning
chopped parsley

Serves **4**
Method
1. Place butter and onions into a glass bowl. Microwave on high for 4 minutes, stirring once.
2. Stir flour and tomato purée into onions then gradually blend in liquids.
3. Add tomatoes then return to microwave, covered and microwave on high for 8 minutes, stirring three times.
4. Liquidise and strain, then season and add grated cheese, microwave on medium for 45 seconds.
5. Serve sprinkled with chopped parsley.

Cream of Lentil Soup

100g (4oz) lentils
1 large carrot, diced
1 medium onion, finely chopped
2 celery stalks, finely chopped
¼ small turnip, diced
50g (2oz) butter
140ml (¼ pint) hot chicken stock
560ml (1 pint) milk
seasoning
1 tablespoon chopped parsley
70ml (⅛ pint) single cream

Serves **4-6**
Method
1. Place lentils into a saucepan with 560ml (1 pint) water and a pinch of salt. Boil on top of cooker for 15 minutes then drain.
2. Place all prepared vegetables into a glass bowl with butter and hot chicken stock. Cover and microwave on high for 16 minutes, stirring every 4 minutes.
3. Place milk into glass jug and microwave on high for 2½ minutes. Blend into vegetables along with lentils, seasoning and parsley. Liquidise.
4. Return mixture to microwave and cook on high for further 8 minutes stirring once. Serve with a swirl of cream.

Chilli Cheeseburgers

450g (1lb) lean minced beef

1 onion, finely chopped

seasoning

$\frac{1}{2}$ teaspoon chilli powder

1 tablespoon soya sauce ⎱

1 tablespoon tomato ketchup ⎰ mixed together

4 slices Scottish cheddar cheese

4 toasted hamburger buns

Method

1. Mix beef, onion, seasoning and chilli powder together with a fork.

2. Divide the mixture into 4 and shape each piece into a burger about 2.5cm (1 inch) thick.

3. Make an indentation in the centre of each with a teaspoon.

4. Arrange evenly on a plate. Brush with soya sauce mixture.

5. Cook for 5-6 minutes turning over and also rotating a $\frac{1}{4}$ turn halfway through cooking.

6. Place hamburgers in buns and top with cheese. Place on a serving dish and cook on high for 1 minute.

7. Serve hot with salad and baked potato.

Mince and Dumplings

450g (1lb) mince

1 large onion, chopped

40g (1½oz) butter

40g (1½oz) plain flour

280ml (½ pint) hot beef stock

140ml (¼ pint) natural yogurt

seasoning

75g (3oz) self raising flour ⎤

40g (1½oz) suet, shredded

50g (2oz) Scottish cheddar ⎬ dumplings
cheese, grated

seasoning

milk to mix ⎦

Serves **4**

Method

1. Place mince, onion and butter into a glass bowl, microwave on high for 6 minutes, stirring once.

2. Stir in flour, seasoning. Blend in hot beef stock. Microwave on high for 6 minutes, stirring twice.

3. Mix in natural yogurt.

4. *Dumpling* — mix all dry ingredients together. Add enough milk to make a firm soft dough.

5. Drop teaspoonfuls of mixture onto mince. Microwave on medium for 12 minutes. Serve.

Chicken Brazil Nut Fricassée

25g (1oz) butter

450g (1lb) chicken breast

1 onion, chopped

75g (3oz) streaky bacon, chopped

150g (6oz) mushrooms, sliced

40g (1½oz) wholemeal flour

420ml (¾ pint) milk

seasoning

50g (2oz) brazil nuts, roughly chopped

Serves **4**

Method

1. Place butter and chicken in a casserole dish. Microwave on high for 7 minutes turning once.

2. Remove chicken from dish and chop into bite sized pieces.

3. Add onion and bacon to chicken juices in casserole and cook on high for 3 minutes.

4. Add flour and gradually stir in milk. Add mushrooms and chicken. Cook for 8 minutes, stirring 4 times.

5. Season to taste. Garnish with chopped brazil nuts.

6. Serve with boiled rice.

Creamy Liver and Bacon

100g (4oz) onion, sliced

1 clove garlic, crushed

75g (3oz) butter

100g (4oz) bacon

340g (12oz) lambs liver

seasoning

2 tablespoons plain flour

140ml (¼ pint) natural yogurt

70ml (⅛ pint) double cream

100g (4oz) mushrooms, sliced

Serves **4**

Method

1. Place onion, garlic, 50g (2oz) butter into a glass bowl. Microwave on high for 2 minutes.

2. Cut bacon into fairly large pieces. Add to onion. Microwave on high for 2 minutes. Keep warm.

3. Cut liver into strips and toss into seasoned flour. Save remaining flour.

4. Place liver in a separate dish along with remaining 25g (1oz) butter, cover and microwave on high for 2 minutes.

5. Add liver to bacon and onion and add 1 dessertspoon of seasoned flour.

6. Blend together yogurt and cream. Stir into liver mixture and add sliced mushrooms, cover. Microwave on high for 6 minutes stirring once. Serve.

Lemon Cheesecake

75g (3oz) butter	base
150g (6oz) wholemeal biscuits	
225g (8oz) low fat soft cheese	filling
1 (size 3) egg, beaten	
1 lemon, rind and juice	
1 teaspoon cornflour	
40g (1½oz) caster sugar	
50g (2oz) sultanas	
little whipped cream for decoration	

Method

1. Place butter in a 18cm (7 inch) flan dish and melt for 1 minute. Stir in biscuits then press evenly into the base and sides of the dish.

2. Beat together all the filling ingredients, then pour into case.

3. Microwave on defrost for 12-16 minutes until the filling is firm round the edges. Leave to stand for 5 minutes. Chill then decorate with whipped cream.

Tipsy Pineapple Caprice

1 egg white

275g (10oz) icing sugar

200g (7oz) tin crushed pineapple, drained well

140ml (¼ pint) double cream, whipped

2 tablespoons Drambuie

To decorate — a little whipped double cream

Serves **4**

Method

1. *Make meringues* — mix egg white and icing sugar to a firm paste.

2. Roll a teaspoonful of the mixture into small balls.

3. Place 6 at a time into a greased bun tray suitable for the microwave. Microwave on high for 1 minute.

4. Leave to stand for 1 minute before carefully turning out.

(This mixture yields approximately 20 meringues. This recipe requires 8 and the remaining meringues can be stored in an airtight container for use later.)

5. *Make caprice* — lightly whip cream and mix in crushed pineapple and Drambuie.

6. Break up meringues and blend into cream mixture.

7. Spoon mixture into 4 individual glasses. Decorate with a swirl of cream and nuts.

8. Serve chilled with sponge fingers.

Orange Velvet

1 packet orange jelly

3 tablespoons water

25g (1oz) drinking chocolate

280ml (½ pint) milk

140ml (¼ pint) natural yogurt

140ml (¼ pint) double cream

Serves **4-6**

Method

1. Break jelly into pieces. Place in a glass bowl along with water. Microwave on high for 1 minute. Stir (jelly should now be dissolved).

2. Stir in drinking chocolate powder until dissolved then whisk in milk.

3. Whip the cream and natural yogurt together until thick.

4. Gradually blend chocolate mixture into cream mixture. Pour into serving dish. Chill for 2-3 hours before serving.

Coconut Eve's Pudding

340g (12oz) cooking apples	
15g (½oz) butter	fruit layer
1 dessertspoon caster sugar	
50g (2oz) butter	
50g (2oz) caster sugar	
1 egg	sponge layer
50g (2oz) self raising flour	
2 tablespoons natural yogurt	
15g (½oz) demerara sugar	topping
15g (½oz) desiccated coconut	

Method

1. *Fruit layer* — peel and core cooking apples. Slice finely into a glass bowl. Add butter. Microwave on high for 3-4 minutes, stirring twice.

2. Add sugar and mix in with a fork. Place fruit mixture in the bottom of an 18cm (7 inch) glass serving bowl.

3. *Sponge layer* — cream together butter and sugar. Add egg and flour beating well, mix in natural yogurt.

4. Spoon on top of fruit and microwave on high for 5 minutes, turning bowl twice. Stand for 4 minutes.

5. *Topping* — mix together coconut and sugar, sprinkle over sponge and serve.

Victoria Sandwich

75g (3oz) butter

75g (3oz) caster sugar

75g (3oz) self raising flour

2 eggs, beaten

2-3 tablespoons milk

Method
1. Cream butter and sugar together.
2. Gradually beat in flour and eggs alternately.
3. Add a little milk until mixture has a soft dropping consistency.
4. Place mixture into 18cm (7 inch) greased microwave ring mould.
5. Microwave on high for 4 minutes, giving a ¼ turn after 2 minutes.
6. Turn out when cooked and leave to stand for 5 minutes, to dry off.
7. Split sponge in half. Fill and decorate with butter icing, as desired.

Syrup Oaties

100g (4oz) butter

100g (4oz) demerara sugar

3 tablespoons syrup

225g (8oz) oats

2 teaspoons cinnamon

2 teaspoons ginger

50g (2oz) raisins

Method
1. Place butter, demerara sugar and syrup into a glass bowl. Microwave on high for 3 minutes, stirring once.
2. Add in the rest of the ingredients.
3. Spoon into 23cm (9 inch) flan dish, flatten slightly.
4. Microwave on high for 4 minutes, turning dish round once.
5. Portion while hot, turn out when cold.

Butter Icing

100g (4oz) butter

150g (6oz) icing sugar, sieved

1-2 tablespoons milk

little vanilla essence

Variations
Lemon — substitute lemon juice for milk and omit vanilla essence.
Chocolate — omit vanilla and add 1 tablespoon cocoa powder.
Coffee — omit vanilla and add 2-3 teaspoons instant coffee powder, dissolved in a little water.
Method
1. Cream butter, then gradually add icing sugar a little at a time along with milk.
2. Add flavouring required.

Basic White Sauce

25g (1oz) flour
25g (1oz) butter
280ml (½ pint) milk
seasoning

Method

1. Melt butter in pan. Blend in flour to make a roux.

3. Gradually blend in milk.

Cheese Sauce

280ml (½ pint) white sauce
75-100g (3-4oz) Scottish cheddar cheese, grated
seasoning
little mustard

Add cheese, seasoning and mustard to white sauce, after sauce has cooked, and stir well.

2. Cook roux for 1 minute, stirring.

4. Return to heat and bring to boil, stirring all the time. Cook for 2-3 minutes. Season.

Tagliatelle Treat

200g (8oz) tagliatelle
560ml (1 pint) white sauce
150g (6oz) Scottish cheddar cheese, grated
150g (6oz) bacon, grilled and chopped
little mustard

Method

1. Boil tagliatelle for 12 minutes and drain.

2. Add cheese, bacon and mustard to sauce and stir.

3. Add tagliatelle and bacon and stir well.

4. Place in ovenproof dish and grill, if desired, with a little extra grated cheese on top.

Shortcrust Pastry

100g (4oz) plain flour
¼ level teaspoon salt
50g (2oz) butter, cut in small pieces
cold water to mix

Oven temperature: 190°C/375°F/No. 5
Position in oven: Centre
Time in oven: 15-20 minutes

Method

1. Sieve flour and salt into bowl. Add butter and rub into flour with fingertips until like fine bread crumbs.

2. Add water and mix in with a round bladed knife.

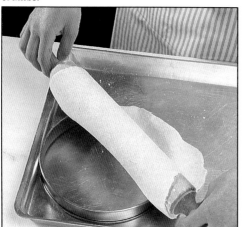

3. Turn out onto a floured board, knead gently and roll out.

4. Line flan ring with pastry. Prick base and bake blind — with no filling. To do this, crumple up some tinfoil and place round edge of flan to stop sides falling in. Remove after half the cooking time.

Quiche

1 × 8 inch cooked shortcrust pastry flan
2 eggs
140ml ($\frac{1}{4}$ pint) milk or cream
75g (3oz) grated cheese
2 tomatoes
seasoning

Oven temperature: 190°C/375°F/No. 5
Position in oven: Centre
Time in oven: 35-40 minutes

Method

1. Beat eggs, add seasoning and milk.

2. Place sliced tomato and $\frac{3}{4}$ of cheese in base of flan.

3. Pour egg mixture into flan and top with rest of cheese.

4. Bake in oven until set.

Crème Caramel

4 eggs	
50g (2oz) sugar	} egg custard
560ml (1 pint) milk	
2 tablespoons water	} caramel
50g (2oz) sugar	

Oven temperature: 150°C/300°F/No. 2
Position in oven: Middle
Time in oven: 1 hour

Method

1. Heat milk to blood heat, add sugar and eggs, beat well.

2. Place water and sugar in a thick pan and heat to caramel colour. Pour into a buttered ovenproof dish which is in a tray with hot water in it.

3. Strain custard mix over caramel and place tray with dish in oven until custard is set.

4. Leave to cool then carefully turn out onto a dish. Serve with fresh fruit salad and cream.

Baked Rice Pudding

50g (2oz) pudding rice

75g (3oz) sugar

560ml (1 pint) milk

little butter

Oven temperature:	190°C/375°F/No. 5
Position in oven:	Middle
Time in oven:	$1\frac{3}{4}$ hours

Method

1. Butter ovenproof dish, wash rice in cold water and place in dish.

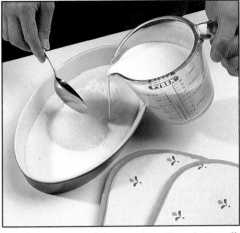

2. Place sugar in dish, pour in milk and stir well.

3. Place in oven and bake for $1\frac{3}{4}$ hours, stirring occasionally.

4. Serve with stewed fruit and fresh cream.

Butter Sponge

100g (4oz) butter
100g (4oz) caster sugar
150g (6oz) self raising flour, sieved
2 eggs, beaten
1-2 dessertspoons hot water

Oven temperature: 190°C/375°F/No. 5
Position in oven: Centre
Time in oven: 25 minutes

Method

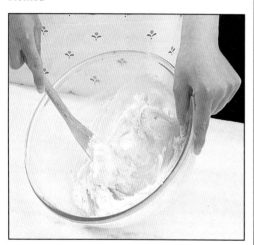

1. Cream butter and sugar thoroughly by hand or mixer.

2. Add eggs and flour alternately.

3. Add hot water to form soft dropping consistency and place in two 18cm (7 inch) buttered tins.

4. Bake in oven until top is golden brown and cake has shrunk slightly away from sides of tins. Decorate with butter icing from recipe on page 85 and coconut.

Egg Sponge

100g (4oz) self raising flour, sieved	
4 eggs	
100g (4oz) caster sugar	
210ml (8oz) whipping cream	} filling
fruit	

Oven temperature:	220°C/425°F/No. 7
Position in oven:	Top half
Time in oven:	10 minutes

Method

1. Whisk eggs and sugar together until creamy with whisk or mixer.

2. Carefully fold in flour.

3. Pour mixture into two 18cm (7 inch) buttered tins.

4. Bake in oven till firm and set. Place on cooling tray. When cold decorate with fresh cream and fruit.

Index